THE COMPLEAT BROWN TROUT

The Compleat Brown Trout

CECIL E. HEACOX

Illustrations by Wayne Trimm

Winchester Press

Library of Congress Catalog Card Number: 73-88873

ISBN: *0–87691–129–7*

Book and jacket design by M. F. Gazze

Published by Winchester Press

460 Park Avenue, New York 10022

Printed in the United States of America

To Dottie, the Compleat Wife
The Finest Catch I Ever Made

Contents

1   FIRST CAST

7   BACK CAST

24   ANATOMY: OUTSIDE

35   ANATOMY: INSIDE

44   SENSES

57   TROPISMS

66   LIFE STYLE

79   ON THE PRODUCTION LINE

92   FOOD

101   MANAGEMENT

117   ECOLOGY

128   TACKLE

144   TACTICS

161   LAST CAST

165   ACKNOWLEDGMENTS

169   BIBLIOGRAPHY

175   INDEX

THE COMPLEAT BROWN TROUT

First Cast

The brown trout is a delight to the eye, exciting to the mind, stimulating to the spirit and delectable to the palate.

In addition to its impeccable credentials in angling circles, the amazing brown trout often shows up in other currents of the mainstream of today's world.

A fish which transcends the conventional concepts

of an ordinary fish. A fish which means different things to different people, and wears its mantle of distinction with grace and flair.

To the dry-fly fisherman, the brown trout is the wariest, wiliest, most fascinating, challenging, respected and best-loved trout of all.

To the ichthyologist, the brown trout, *Salmo trutta* Linnaeus, is viewed from the detached point of view of the scientist—not in the angler's images of action, but as a zoological specimen: a cold-blooded vertebrate, breathing by means of gills, limbs developed as fins, streamlined, a showcase model of perfect adaptation to life in the water.

To the ecologist, the brown trout is a significant indicator organism, attesting to an environmental quality also favorable to man.

To an artist like Wayne Trimm, with his sensitivity for faithful anatomical structure and feeling for dramatic action, the brown trout is as exciting to capture on canvas as in the stream—as challenging to the brush as to the rod.

To the musician Franz Schubert, the brown trout was inspiration. His enduring composition *Die Forelle* ("The Trout") is a masterpiece of charm and delight, rippling like a mountain brook in Schubert's native Austria. Composed in 1819, *Die Forelle* has stood the test of time in the world of music, as has the trout in the angling world.

To the master chef Auguste Escoffier, the brown trout was also inspiration. It is the key ingredient in one of his culinary triumphs, *Truite au bleu*—an epicurean masterpiece which delights the palates of gourmets the world over. "The best," said Escoffier, "are those procured in mountain districts where the clear water they inhabit is constantly refreshed by currents."

To the American businessman, the brown trout is part of a multibillion-dollar market made up of over fifty million fishermen. In the United States, the introduction of the brown trout revolutionized the design and construction of the tools of the trade: the advent of the dry fly; a different action in fly rods; new editions of reels; new kinds of lines. Dry-fly fishing for brown trout can become a many-splendored thing.

To the historian, the odyssey of *Salmo trutta* spins a fascinating adventure story. Originally native to Europe and sections of Asia and Africa, the brown trout was transplanted to other regions of the globe. Today thriving populations of brown trout stir up excitement in the fishing waters of every part of the world except Antarctica.

To the bookish angler, the brown trout is a leading character in a stream of several thousand fishing books. Strangely enough, though, there have been less than a dozen volumes devoted exclusively to the brown trout—and none in America.

In the third century, Claudius Aelianus,[1] a Roman nature writer, not only described for the first time the brown trout—"the fish with speckled skins"—but also gave an account of fly fishing during a mayfly hatch on the River Astraeus in Macedonia.

From Britain, twelve hundred years later—perhaps anglers were enjoying fishing too much to write about it—came the first book about fishing in the English language: *Treatyse of Fysshynge wyth an Angle*, attributed to the legendary Juliana Berners,[2] of the nunnery of Sopwell at the Abbey of St. Albans.

After the *Treatyse* there was a lapse of a century. Then four fishing books in English came from the pens of Leonard Mascall,[3] Gervase Markham,[4] William Lawson,[5] and Thomas Barker,[6] all obviously influenced by Dame Juliana. Also the first fishing book in verse by

John Dennys.[7] I was allowed to hold and reverently read the British Museum's rare first edition of 1613.

In 1653 came the first edition of *The Compleat Angler* by Izaak* Walton.[8] To Walton and Dame Juliana the brown trout was simply "the trout"—the only trout they knew. Both, of course, wrote about species other than the trout, but who remembers their discourses on the barbel, the tench or the bream?

Walton reveals himself as less of a fly fisherman than Juliana Berners, but this shortcoming was corrected by Charles Cotton in 1676 when he contributed Part II to *The Compleat Angler:* a specialized treatment of fly fishing for brown trout, with a list of sixty-five flies, the dressing instructions much the same as a modern flytier would give them.

Walton hardly could have foreseen that his slim book—the original edition made to fit the pocket of a fishing jacket—would run into nearly four hundred editions. With more to come, no doubt.

Since Walton's time a spate of several thousand fishing books have rolled off the presses, hundreds devoted to fly fishing, in which the brown trout emerges in a leading role.

In 1841, George P. R. Pulman,[9] based in Devonshire's brown-trout region, first floated the dry fly in angling literature. A half century later, Pulman's countryman, Frederic M. Halford[10] of the chalk stream coun-

4
The Compleat Brown Trout

⌐✳

---

*Walton was named "Isaac" by his parents, and his name is so spelled on his gravestone in Winchester Cathedral. But he did not like the name—anyone named "Cecil" is sympathetic—and changed it to "Izaak," even signing his will that way. His preference for "Izaak" was honored in 295 editions of *The Compleat Angler;* only 40 have the "Isaac" byline. Other variations include "Izaac" in 22 editions and "Isaak" in 5 editions. At first I thought it might be more scholarly and authentic to use "Isaac," but later changed my mind. I think Izaak would have wanted it that way.

try, secured lasting status for the theory and practice of angling for the brown trout with the dry fly.

Although there has been no American book exclusively devoted to *Salmo trutta* since it was introduced into our waters in 1883, most books on fly fishing give the brown trout top billing. Indeed, George M. L. La Branche,[11] whose *The Dry Fly and Fast Water* continues as a classic on this side of the Atlantic, declared that "the original reason for writing the book was the brown trout."

To me, as an angler, boy and man, my kinship with the brown trout has been a long and happy love affair. Glistening gold and flecked with bright red spots, the prettiest fish I had ever seen, my first brown trout came from the Rondout, a jewel of a stream in New York's Catskill Mountains. It is a region interlaced with beautiful trout streams, including the hallowed Beaver Kill.

That unforgettable brown trout was also my first trout. A commonplace enough happening to a young fisherman today. But in 1910, the Rondout was a brook-trout stream; browns were just beginning to take hold.

About the same time, on the Neversink, a sister stream in the next valley, Theodore Gordon,[12] influenced by Frederic Halford, had already established himself as the chief architect of dry-fly fishing in America and founder of the "Catskill School of Flytiers."

Soon the brown trout/dry-fly mystique spread from New York's Beaver Kill to Vermont's Batten Kill, Pennsylvania's Brodheads, Michigan's Ausable, Wisconsin's Wolf, Wyoming's Firehole, Montana's Madison and hundreds of less famous streams across America.

Since the day I caught my first brown trout, I've caught many others. And learned something from them all—each adding to my respect for and enchantment with this superb sporting fish.

The time is long overdue in acknowledging my debt to such a distinguished quarry.

This treatise is for all who esteem a magnificent creation of nature; for those who do their fishing in books as well as brooks.

He who fishes for facts also reaps rewards. Hopefully, a better notion of what makes a brown trout tick will launch anglers on new adventures. To a growing legion of dry-fly fishermen, a better understanding brings a closer rapport with the noble brown; a reward savored long after leaving the stream.

So salute to *Salmo trutta*. To the brown trout. With appreciation, respect and love, these words come from the heart.

The Compleat Brown Trout

Back Cast

On its own the brown trout has been on the move since the last ice age. With the help of man, *Salmo trutta*'s range has been enlarged so it is now found in waters of every continent on the planet except Antarctica.

The brown trout has what it takes for successful survival: adaptability and a personality to dominate its environment.

8
The Compleat
Brown Trout

⊰⋇

With the brown trout's strong hankering for cold-water habitats, scientists presume that the brown trout first surfaced as a migratory fish of the Arctic regions during the Eocene Epoch, seventy million years ago.

When the vast ice sheet spread southward at the beginning of the Glacial Epoch, brown trout swam ahead of it, establishing new homes in inland lakes and streams.

Later, the seas gradually warmed up as the glacier retreated. Populations of brown trout remained in the streams and lakes they had entered, establishing new habitats for *Salmo trutta*. Apparently the more accomplished travelers—brown trout endowed with a stronger wanderlust—migrated back to their home in the Arctic region. Other population units preferred the seas which had helped them survive during the Glacial Epoch, becoming what we know as sea trout: sea-run browns returning each year to freshwater streams to spawn.

Thus, by a fortunate roll of the geological dice, colonies of brown trout became established in the fjords of Norway, *Salmo trutta*'s original home around the Arctic; the burns and lochs of Scotland; in the chalk streams of England; across Europe—France, Germany, Austria—to the brawling rivers of Yugoslavia; to the tributaries of the Caspian Sea; across Russia to Asia and the Hindu Kush on the western edge of the Himalayas; south in Europe to the Pyrenees of Spain; and across the Mediterranean to the Atlas streams of Algeria and Morocco in North Africa. Offshoot populations became established in Corsica and Sardinia.

Throughout its widespread range, the brown trout became a respected resident and much sought-after fish. As Izaak Walton noted: "The trout is a fish highly valued in this and foreign nations."

The brown trout was further spread by man, and

especially by British colonialism. Like other hallmark products of the British Isles, it was exported to all parts of the Empire.

When Englishmen ventured into the midday sun of far-off places, their favorite sports went with them. Along with London gin and Scotch whisky, cricket bats and polo mallets, fishing rods were invariably part of their baggage bound for India, South Africa or Australia.

To a devout British trout fisherman, fishing is simply not fishing unless the quarry is his beloved brown trout. In India, for instance, a popular native fish, *Notopenis notopenis,* was accepted as a table delicacy—or in soup a cure for measles—but it was not much on the end of a fishing line.

In every corner of the far-flung British Empire, anglers became homesick for the sporting brown trout of the Test, the Itchen and other holy angling waters back home. Fated by geography, transplanted English sportsmen dreamed of also transplanting their favorite fish to the waters around their outpost stations.

British enterprise tackled the problem with typical bulldog persistence. Australia's temperate climate, something like Britain's, was a logical choice for an opener. But it turned out to be the toughest target, because of the seemingly impossible task of getting fish eggs through the heat of the tropics and across the equator in the slow ships of the time.

Attempts to transplant salmon eggs to Australia were made in 1852, 1858 and 1860. Although complete failures, these sporadic attempts were a prelude to a breakthrough. The experiments demonstrated that the key to successful egg transport was a sufficient supply of ice. Adequately refrigerated to a temperature of 33–35° F., the incubation period of eggs could be prolonged for a voyage of 150 days or more.

9
Back Cast

WORLD DISTRIBUTION OF BROWN TROUT

Original distribution

Successful introduction

Cargo space in the hold being much too valuable to store the amount of ice needed, these persistent pioneers decided to build an ice house on the lowest deck.

In January 1864, the *Norfolk*, built for steam but clipper-rigged for this voyage, with an ice house holding 30 tons, sailed out of Falmouth for Australia with 90,000 salmon eggs. Through last-minute efforts of Frank Buckland and Francis Francis, two notable names in British angling circles, 1,500 brown trout eggs—mostly from one pair of River Itchen trout—were added to the shipment. These brown trout eggs had a rendezvous with destiny.

On April 15, the *Norfolk* reached Melbourne. About 30,000 salmon eggs were still alive. After hatching, the fry were stocked, but a century later there is no evidence that the fry survived.

Three hundred brown-trout eggs survived the journey. Part of the batch stayed in Melbourne, and some were sent to Hobart, Tasmania, and placed in a hatchery supplied by water from the Plenty River.

The first brown trout eggs in Down Under waters began hatching on May 4, 1864. At the beginning of 1866, 171 of the original batch of brown trout eggs were thriving in hatchery ponds, a demonstration of the strong survival instinct of *Salmo trutta*. Thirty-eight were planted in the Plenty River. During the winter—July and August in the Antipodes—these brown trout spawned in the river, the first natural reproduction of brown trout below the equator. After 1868 the Plenty River became an excellent natural breeding stream and a source of supply for other Tasmanian streams, waters of the Australian mainland and New Zealand.

In their new ecological niche in Tasmania, the immigrants, taking advantage of an abundant and unused food supply, grew to prodigious sizes.

A 40-pound brown trout from Tasmania long held the record for the largest brown taken by any method, a record which apparently has been topped by a 56-pound fish from Yugoslavia. The world's angling record—39 pounds, 8 ounces—from Loch Awe, Scotland, was established in 1866.

Some years ago, G. C. Cramp, A Tasmanian fish commissioner, wrote me reporting a good season: 662 brown trout, one-third of the catch weighing over 3 pounds.

Plenty River brown trout eggs were shipped to New Zealand's South Island in 1868, marking the beginning of one of the world's finest brown trout paradises. Globe-trotting anglers have described the Maturi River on South Island as the world's greatest brown trout dry-fly stream.

Africa was the next challenge on the transplanting agenda. Colin Fletcher[13] quotes Lord Delamere, founder of white settlement in East Africa: "What white settlers will want to find here," said Delamere to a friend, "is wheat in their fields and trout in their rivers. You fix the trout and I'll look after the wheat."

The first shipment of brown trout eggs went out from Britain to South Africa's Cape Province in 1875. Another shipment followed in 1882. Both attempts were failures. In 1884, a shipment made the trip but succumbed to zinc poisoning from hatchery trough linings. The first successful venture in Cape Province was in 1892. Earlier—1890—brown trout were introduced into the Bushmans, Mooi and Umgeni rivers of Natal. At first these efforts appeared to be failures, but around 1900, brown trout were found to be well established.

Farther north on the African continent, Kenya, more famous for big-game hunting, got its start with brown trout through the heroic efforts of Lord Delamere's friend Major Ewart Grogan, noted for his two-year walk from Cape Town to Cairo.

At his own expense, Major Grogan, in 1905, brought in both German and Loch Leven stock. The eggs survived a 7,000-mile sea journey, including the torrid Red Sea; 400 miles of rail travel; and finally a long, tortuous trek on porters' heads to a primitive mountain hatchery.

14
The Compleat
Brown Trout

By 1909, these fish began to show up in anglers' creels—the beginning of Kenya's fabulous brown-trout fishing. Here, practically on the equator at elevations to 15,000 feet, brooks in the Aberdare Mountains and streams spilling down Mt. Kenya were practically devoid of fish before brown trout were introduced. *Salmo trutta* has a talent for filling previously unused ecological niches.

Some British anglers make journeys to Kenya for brown-trout fishing as many American sportsmen now go to Africa for big-game safaris. Colin Fletcher once philosophized: "Should some evil chance restrict all my fishing to one place . . . I'd pick a certain small brown trout stream in the Kenya Highlands. The fish are small; they average perhaps half a pound. But every inch of that stream is different, every inch is fly water. And each of those little trout is an individual that has to be selected, stalked and overcome . . . to me, it typifies brown trout fishing at its best."

That capsule reverie strikes a responsive chord in the angling soul of thousands of fishermen who search out the brown trout with a dry fly in every part of the world.

Today, it seems to require a delegate to the United Nations to keep abreast of the names of the new African nations. Tanzania—Tanganyika to those of us who studied geography before the World Wars—Uganda, Malawi, Rhodesia and others have tried to introduce brown trout, with indifferent success compared to Kenya. A stocking in 1926 resulted in a naturalized stock of brown trout on the island of Madagascar.

India was another early target for brown-trout introductions. The Himalayas, roof of the world, halted the eastward spread of brown trout at the end of the last ice age. *Salmo trutta* lived in some of the lakes and streams of the Hindu Kush but not in the waters of India on the eastern side. In 1866, an unsuccessful attempt was made to establish brown trout in Madras, but another try two years later succeeded. Here, Loch Levens, in time, developed the red spots of German stock.

The Hindu Kush barrier was hurdled when in 1900 the Duke of Bedford sent the Maharajah of Kashmir a present of brown-trout eggs in exchange for several Kashmir stags. This shipment did not survive, but another consignment later the same year and another the next year did. In time, back-scratching *noblesse oblige* paid off. Kashmir brown-trout fishing is well known throughout the angling world. Retired British colonials make sentimental journeys back to Kashmir just for the brown trout fishing.

Later, Kashmir stock was used to establish brown-trout populations in Punjab and other waters in northern India.

A shipment of brown trout eggs from the United States to Japan in 1892 resulted in the establishment of the species in Chuzenji Lake, Tochigi.

Nearly two decades after the brown trout began its modern man-assisted odyssey, the great game fish was introduced to America. A chance meeting and a simple fishing trip started the brown trout on its way.

In 1880, the International Fisheries Exposition was held in Berlin. Fred Mather, fisherman, fish culturist,

A canvass (1972) of the United States regarding original introductions of brown trout produced a response from all fifty
states.

The U.S. Fish Commission stocked many waters throughout the
United States with brown trout before and after state agencies were
established—records which may or may not be in state files. Mac-
Crimmon and Marshall (1968) and MacCrimmon, Marshall, and
Gots (1970) listed introductions based chiefly on U.S. Fish Com-
mission reports.

The author has used only dates furnished by the states. Dates in
roman type were successful introductions; those in italic type were
unsuccessful. Some dates are approximate. In states for which no
dates appear, no introduction has been attempted.

16
*The Compleat
Brown Trout*

State, etc.	Year
Alabama	*c. 1942*
Alaska	—
Arizona	1924
Arkansas	1949
California	1894
Colorado	1903
Connecticut	1893
Delaware	1968
Florida	—
Georgia	c. 1900
Hawaii	*1935*
Idaho	1918
Illinois	c. 1900
Indiana	c. 1900
Iowa	c. 1900
Kansas	—
Kentucky	—
Louisiana	—
Maine	1885
Maryland	1929
Massachusetts	1887
Michigan	1883
Minnesota	1888

Mississippi	—
Missouri	1966
Montana	1889
Nebraska	1889
Nevada	1930
New Hampshire	1887
New Jersey	1912
New Mexico	1926
New York	1883
North Carolina	c. 1900
North Dakota	1954
Ohio	*c. 1900*
Oklahoma	—
Oregon	1897
Pennsylvania	1886
Rhode Island	1940
South Carolina	c. 1900
South Dakota	1891
Tennessee	c. 1900
Texas	—
Utah	1895
Vermont	1892
Virginia	1960
Washington	c. 1933
West Virginia	c. 1930
Wisconsin	1887
Wyoming	1890
Puerto Rico	*1938*
Alberta	1924
British Columbia	1933
Manitoba	1943
New Brunswick	1921
Newfoundland	1886
Nova Scotia	1925
Ontario	1913
Prince Edward Island	—
Quebec	1890
Saskatchewan	1924
Northwest Territories	—
Yukon	—

17
Back Cast

fishing writer, was a United States delegate. Over a glass of pilsner, Mather met Baron Lucius von Behr, a German delegate and president of a German fishing society—Deutscher Fischerei Verein. The acquaintance ripened into a warm friendship.

Baron von Behr invited his new friend to fish some of the Black Forest streams. Mather, an ardent angler, needed no arm-twisting. The Black Forest browns, like their relatives today, cast their magic spell, putting on a performance which has warmed the hearts of anglers since the days of Aelianus, Berners and Walton.

Fred Mather's enthusiasm for *Salmo trutta* also worked a little magic. Baron von Behr promised to send Mather a batch of brown trout eggs as a gift.

The Baron did not forget. He sent several shipments, in fact, to the United States. The first shipment—the gift to Mather—arrived in New York in February 1883. Mather retained part of the batch at the newly completed New York State hatchery at Cold Spring Harbor, Long Island, where he was now in charge. Part of the shipment was sent to a sister state hatchery at Caledonia, and the remainder went to the United States Fish Commission's hatchery at Northville, Michigan.

Some of the Northville fry were stocked in Michigan's Père Marquette River, giving the Père Marquette the honor of being the first major trout stream in America to be stocked with brown trout.

The following year, eggs of the Loch Leven strain from Scotland's Howietoun hatchery came to the United States. At first the German stock and the Loch Leven strain showed the typical distinguishing differences: the trout with the golden-hued body and bright-red spots was known as the German brown trout or the von Behr trout; the trout with the silvery sheen and lacking the red spots, the Loch Leven. For many years, state and federal fish-distribution records listed both Loch Leven trout and von Behr trout. In time, both in the wild and in hatcheries, the two strains became so mixed that the original distinguishing characteristics gradually disappeared.

During World War I, in a burst of well-meaning patriotism, everything "German" was dropped from our language, and the German brown trout became generally known simply as the brown trout.

Soon after brown trout were introduced into the United States, fish culturists went on a colossal stocking binge. From Maine to California, all sizes and ages of brown trout—from eggs to adults—were planted on a wholesale scale. By 1900, brown trout had been stocked in thirty-eight states. They were stocked in Arizona and New Mexico when they were still territories, and in Montana in 1889 and Wyoming in 1900, getting off to a good start the year statehood was achieved.

The early fish culturists operated on the principle that "the more fish you put in, the more fish you will take out." Little was known, so little consideration was given to species suitability and the carrying capacity of waters.

The effects of this wholesale stocking were soon evident. To the brown trout, America was a land of opportunity, as it was to so many other immigrants of that era. The result: a population explosion.

Demonstrating its typical adaptability, the brown trout took a firm hold on the American angling scene, showing a remarkable capacity for thriving under conditions which the native brook trout could not tolerate. Even under ideal conditions for brook trout, the browns' strong personality soon dominated. With a no-nonsense, take-charge posture the brown became the boss of nearly every pool, riff and spawning bed. The brook trout retreated to the headwaters of the colder streams.

Trout fishermen who had established reputations filling their creels with brook trout found the brown a different breed of fish. They discovered that the brown trout is often difficult and sometimes impossible to catch.

Unlike British anglers, who gratefully welcomed the brown trout wherever it was established in colonial waters, frustrated American fishermen greeted the immigrant with contempt.

"Just a speckled carp," some sneered.

"A cannibal," claimed others when they found trout in brown trout stomachs.

"They don't taste good," declared self-acclaimed gourmets.

Not a word, of course, from fishermen confessing they had met their match; not a word about angling's exciting, new challenge of a hard-to-catch fish.

In 1897, the Michigan Conservation Commission, clobbered by hosts of irate fishermen, concluded: "A few years of experiment and experience have convinced us that the brown trout is inferior in every respect to the brook or rainbow."

Later, State of Montana officials came closer to the truth: "The brown trout is a good fish, but the average angler is not skilled enough to catch it."

In Maine, where not only brook trout but the land-locked salmon have often yielded to the more aggressive brown, the case was stated in thrifty Yankee fashion: "Brown trout are a poor investment in terms of returns to the fisherman."

Apparently some of the brown trout's dominating personality rubbed off on Fred Mather. During the uproar, he stoutly defended the trout he helped bring to America:

"Some anglers have objected to the introduction of the brown trout in our streams because they grow too fast and might eventually kill our native fish. To this I say, 'Let 'em do it if they can and the fittest will survive' . . . a trout is a cannibal when he gets to be three years old whether he is a native or an adopted citizen and it is only a question of which fish matures in the shortest time for the angler."

In Canada, introductions of brown trout began soon after they started in the United States.

Fish culturists in the United States and Canada were getting to know each other at the meetings of the American Fisheries Society, an organization founded in 1870 and still going strong. Professional courtesy in the tradition of the Duke of Bedford and the Maharajah of Kashmir prevailed in its membership, resulting in exchanges of eggs between hatcheries, states and provinces on the North American continent.

The earliest Canadian record, 1886, shows an import of 100,000 Loch Leven eggs to Newfoundland, where they were incubated in a small hatchery built by the Game Fish Protection Society of St. Johns. After hatching, the fry were planted in waters around St. Johns, mainly in the tributaries of Quidi Vidi Lake.

In 1890, brown trout fry from New York's Caledonia Hatchery were stocked in Lac Brule, Quebec. A big Lac Brule brown, caught in 1897, has been claimed as the first brown trout taken by angling in Canadian waters.

In 1921, 23,000 fry and fingerlings, also from Caledonia, were stocked in Loch Lomond, New Brunswick, marking the beginning of fine brown trout sport fishing in the Maritimes.

Other records of brown trout introductions into Dominion waters include: Alberta, 1924; Ontario, 1913;

Saskatchewan, 1924; British Columbia, 1933; Manitoba, 1943; Nova Scotia, 1925. The Province of Prince Edward Island, the Northwest Territories and the Yukon Territory have not yet attempted to introduce brown trout.

The reactions of Canadian anglers and government agencies to the brown trout had a familiar ring. A few years ago I received a note from a Newfoundland fisheries official: "The spread of the brown trout . . . shows definite progress all along the Coastline . . . it has been my prediction for some time that within twenty-five years, the brown trout will have replaced the char [brook trout]. This is not a pleasant prospect as generally the brown trout does not have either the fishing or eating qualities of the char."

At the other end of the Western Hemisphere, eggs from German hatcheries successfully crossed the equator to Argentina in 1904 and to Chile in 1905.

As a native of the Arctic regions, the brown trout has come a long way from its original home and is now getting close to Antarctica. Tierra del Fuego, at the tip of Argentina, is the southernmost limit of brown trout fishing in the world. Tierra del Fuego offers resident brown-trout fishing and spectacular sea trout fishing— trout so big some anglers use tarpon flies.

MacCrimmon and others,[14] in an intensive review of the world distribution of *Salmo trutta*, report the successful introduction of the species in Peru (1928) and the Falkland Islands (1947). Naturalized populations have also become established in Bolivia and Venezuela. The brown trout has become the true international fish.

Meanwhile, back in the United States, a funny thing was happening on the way to the trout stream.

As fishermen became better acquainted with Fred Mather's adopted citizen, resentment began to subside. Gradually *Salmo trutta* was accepted, then respected,

22
The Compleat Brown Trout

then admired and finally appreciated. What was once a question-mark fish is now an exclamation-point fish.

As the quality of America's aquatic environments deteriorated, renewed hope was pinned on the brown trout to save trout fishing.

Of the forty-two states in which brown trout have been introduced into public waters, fishing is now enjoyed in thirty-eight. Arkansas, Delaware, Missouri and North Dakota have joined the ranks of brown trout states since World War II.

Missouri, after an abortive attempt in 1930, tried again in 1966. As a result both the North Fork (White River) and the Current River provide trophy brown trout fishing.

Arkansas, after futile attempts to establish brown trout in the decade before 1900, strived to beef up its put-and-take fishing with plantings of brown trout in 1949 and 1952. As a result several resident populations have become established, chiefly in the White River, which has yielded some big browns that have won awards in national fishing contests, including a giant of 31 pounds 8 ounces, the present Arkansas state record.

As recently as 1972, Kentucky and Texas were considering experimental plantings in selected waters.

As Dr. James R. Westman,[15] fellow alumnus of the New York State Biological Survey, university professor and angling author, has stated: "The brown trout is one of the most perfectly suited water animals ever introduced to the North American continent."

And so the odyssey of the brown trout continues. *Salmo trutta* has come a long way since Aelianus, in the third century, wrote about "the fish with speckled skins." A fish with a heritage of many million years and a future destined to burn brightly for years to come—a fish which wears its yesterdays with honor and its todays with glory.

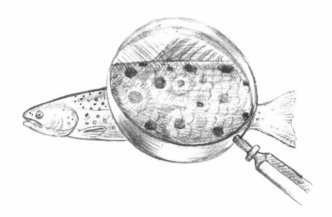

Anatomy: Outside

Early in my conservation career, I was asked to give a talk to an elite fishing club—a club where the brown trout and dry-fly fishing are a religion and streams like the Catskill's Beaver Kill and Neversink are sacrosanct.

Bemused by several preprandial martinis and a smug scientific knowledge recently acquired as a graduate student at Cornell University under Dr. George C. Embody, the dean of American ichthyologists in the 1930s, I referred to the brown trout as a low form of fish life. Quicker than you can say "Quill Gordon," a wounded look appeared on the faces of the group around the table. Immediately I realized I should have used the word "primitive." There were some strained moments. But apparently my own admiration for *Salmo trutta* came through and helped restore my image.

The brown trout is put in the primitive category because its long and honorable family history dates back seventy million years ago to the Eocene Period of the Cenozoic Era.

Structurally, too, the brown trout has a body construction that passed the survival test several geologic ages ago: a smooth naked head and a fusiform body—the scientists' term for a slightly compressed spindle shape, ideal for rapid movements in water.

The body is covered with cycloid scales and smooth to the touch, resembling fingerprints under magnification. The scales are like fingernails, nourished at the roots by cells which throw off the material of which the scale is made.

Running along the side of a brown trout, from head to tail, is the lateral line, which further carries out a streamlining effect. The lateral line functions primarily as a hearing aid.

A very thin skin, almost invisible, covers the scales. It is formed of living cells which exude mucus, reducing friction and helping the trout to move through the water with its lightning speed. This mucus also helps to prevent fungus and resists bacterial and parasitic infections.

Mucus performs an even more vital function. The skin is a semi-permeable membrane, and the brown

EXTERNAL ANATOMY OF THE BROWN TROUT
(see also Color Plate II)

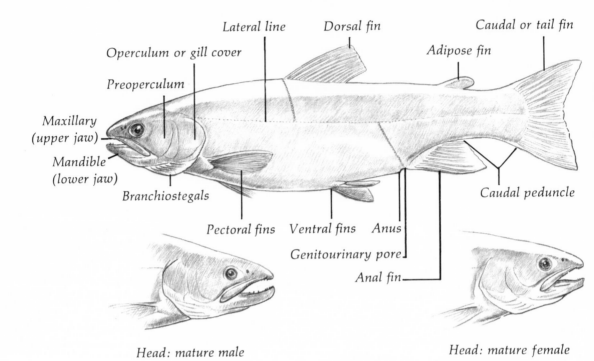

Head: mature male

Head: mature female

trout's internal fluids are slightly salty. Thus in fresh water, a trout would eventually absorb enough water to become waterlogged if the process were not slowed up by the skin's protective coating of mucus.

When *Salmo trutta* goes to salt water as a sea trout, this process is reversed, because sea water has a much higher salt content than the internal fluids of the trout. If it were not for the mucus, the internal machinery of the sea trout would soon dry up.

Attached to the brown trout's body is a complement of eight fins: anal, tail, dorsal, adipose and two sets of paired fins—the pectoral fins behind the gills and the ventral or pelvic fins attached to the belly.

The tail fin of young brown trout is slightly forked.

In older browns, the tail becomes nearly square, occasionally fan-shaped.

In cold, pedantic prose, textbooks equate the fins of a fish with locomotion—especially the tail, which in sweeping from side to side pushes the water backward and the trout forward. The tail also acts as a rudder.

The dorsal, anal and to some extent the adipose fins serve as keels, preventing yawing and rolling; the paired pectorals and ventrals perform as brakes, stabilizers and auxiliary rudders.

For a long time, as practically all of the textbooks stated, it was assumed that the fins were the only means of locomotion. In my researching I came across an account which boldly stated that a fish is able to navigate after all its fins have been cut off. The statement raised my eyebrows, some strong doubts and an urge to make a test case.

As a fisheries biologist I had marked over 100,000 brown trout by clipping various fins as an identification mark in checking on migration, survival and growth of plantings of hatchery-raised browns. Usually I clipped just one fin but never more than two, one of which was invariably the small adipose fin. These trout survived and thrived. But removing *all* fins was a different kettle of fish. However, I was sure if any fish could survive fin clipping it was the brown trout.

With the hope of finding the answer, I enlisted the help of a former colleague, Neil F. Ehlinger, fish pathologist at the New York State Fish Pathology Laboratory at Rome, New York. Neil succeeded Dr. Louis E. Wolf, one of my early mentors, who was one of the world's first fish pathologists and established the Rome Laboratory.

Neil and I had some qualms about the harshness of the experiment, which was excused, if not exactly in the name of science, on the grounds of obtaining a better understanding of a brown trout's swimming abilities.

At Cornell, Neil and I were strongly influenced by our teacher, Dr. Embody, who frequently pointed out that the more you know about a fish the more you will enjoy fishing for it—a statement that continues to ring a bell with me each succeeding fishing season.

In spite of the general opinion that fish do not feel pain as humans do, the trout were heavily anesthetized. In the recovery tank, the totally fin-clipped browns at first showed a wobbling motion in forward movements, but total imbalance was not observed. Indeed, the trout soon showed an amazing ability to adjust to their handicap.

When placed in a trough of running water—current 10 feet per second—the trout still maintained themselves in a normal swimming position but with accentuated body movement, the caudal peduncle substituting for a tail. Except for this noticeable extra effort, the clipped trout maintained themselves in a fashion similar to their tank companions, equipped with a full complement of fins. Later, the totally clipped trout were put in an aquarium and started feeding at once.

One test like this, of course, is not a scientific experiment. In the wild, a brown trout without fins would probably find it difficult to compete with other fishes or would become easy prey to predators.

However, the trial run did demonstrate conclusively that the great mass of motive force—the major thrust of locomotion—is contained in the body muscles.

As the brown trout becomes a free-swimming fry, parr marks—nine to ten dark, vertical bars—form on its sides. Parr marks fade gradually, usually disappearing when the trout reaches fingerling size. Parr marks are a sign of immaturity, possibly like the acne of an adolescent boy. Occasionally, however, parr marks remain throughout the life of a brown trout.

As the male brown trout reaches sexual maturity, a hook forms on the lower jaw, more noticeable in older trout and especially pronounced at spawning time. This character gives the brown a pugnacious look to match its stubborn fighting qualities.

Over three centuries ago, Izaak Walton described the brown trout: "The very shape and the enamelled colour of him hath been such as hath joyed me to look on him."

Walton's nice bit of poetic imagery still holds. Actually, however, the brown trout does not have a standardized appearance. Throughout its range, original and adopted, a brown's color pattern varies in different locales and habitats; sometimes from stream to stream and, not infrequently, in the same stream. In addition, a well-developed accommodation for protective coloration—one of the many tricks that fool the angler—enables a brown to blend perfectly with a light sandy bottom or the floor of a forest stream darkened by a closed canopy of trees.

Salmo trutta, however, is called the brown trout for the obvious reason—an inherent color pattern associated with a shade of brown: hues of olive, bronze or yellow on the back and sides above the lateral line. Below the lateral line, a distinct color change usually takes place, varying from a lighter shade of the color above the line to gold or tawny, to gray, silver, cream or white.

Spots of red and black, often framed in a halo of blue, dot the back and sides above the lateral line with a scattering of more widely separated spots below the line.

With few exceptions, such as the black-finned strain of Wales or residents of murky bog ponds in

America, a brown trout's fins are a shade of yellow. The dorsal fin is marked with a few dark spots, sometimes a reddish tint; the margin of the anal fin is unspotted and edged with white outside a fine line of black. The tail fin and the paired pectorals and ventrals are also unspotted. The adipose fin is dotted with spots of red, orange or brown; its rim is also fringed with one of these shades.

This touch of color in the adipose fin is a fairly reliable character for identifying wild browns. No other member of the trout and salmon family has it.

In my hatchery days, meat was included in brown trout diets, and color in the adipose began to show in the fry stage of development. However, I've noticed that in hatcheries where manufactured pellets constitute the brown trout's food, the color character does not show up at any stage in the product rolling off the assembly line.

However, the brown's most reliable identification character—distinguishing it from brooks, rainbows and landlocked salmon—are the well-developed vomerine teeth on the raised shaft of bone in the center of the mouth, arranged in distinctive double-zigzag rows.

But even what seem to be clean-cut characters are frequently puzzling, and the recognition of closely related varieties of salmonoids is often extremely difficult.

Because the brown trout varies so much in its habitats in different parts of the world, both fishermen and scientists have regarded many of the varieties as separate species. Besides the handsome trout of his beloved Lea, Izaak Walton mentions the Fordidge trout of Kent, the Bull-trout of Northumberland and the Salmon-trout. In some lakes of Ireland, the brown trout may masquerade as a "gillaroo," a strain with a thick-walled stomach, caused, it seems, by a steady diet of

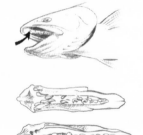

Vomerine teeth

snails and shellfish. In this country when I was a very young angler, Loch Leven, German brown and von Behr trout were part of the fisherman's language. Mostly, the common names for brown trout stem from geographical location: Dalmatian trout, Hungarian trout, Caspian trout and so on.

The sea trout in Great Britain has many aliases, based sometimes on location and sometimes on age, as: Galway trout, Orkney trout, sewin, phinnock, peal, whitling, herling and truff. In New England, sea-run browns are known as "salters" or "coasters," confusing because Down Easters apply these same names to sea-run native brook trout.

Common names for animals and plants are often unsatisfactory because they may mean different things to different people. The early naturalists struggled to create a more scientific nomenclature, attempts which culminated in 1758 with the publication of the *Systema Naturae* of Carl Linnaeus.[16]

Employing a combination of genera and species, Linnaeus' new binomial system was hailed as the answer to the taxonomist's prayer, a perfect filing cabinet for all of nature's creations.

In classifying the brown trout, Linnaeus started modestly enough, putting three species in his file—species with which he had a firsthand acquaintance in his native Sweden: *Salmo fario,* the trout of small brooks; *Salmo trutta,* the trout of large rivers; and *Salmo eriox,* the sea trout.

During the next century, naturalists, working independently in their own countries and probably with little communication with colleagues, were assigning their own original scientific names to what they regarded as a new species of trout.

Consequently in 1864, when Dr. Albert C. L. G.

31
Anatomy:
Outside

Günther[17] completed the gigantic task of classifying and cataloguing the specimens of fishes which had been presented to the British Museum, the brown trout had acquired an amazing number of scientific titles.

Commenting on the genus *Salmo*, Dr. Günther said resignedly: "We know of no other group of fishes which offers so many difficulties to ichthyologists with regard to the distinction of the species."

Dr. Günther ended up his cataloguing job with eighty-three species of the genus *Salmo*. For the British Isles alone, ten different species of brown trout. Of the eighty-three species, probably thirty or so are today considered the brown trout.

On a recent London visit, in addition to checking brown trout literature, I had the opportunity of examining many of the specimens of *Salmo* over which Dr. Günther labored with such devotion.

All specimens had long ago lost any trace of color. Yet, without checking the label, many specimens have a familiar look to American trout fishermen. Certainly, *Salmo levenensis* of Scotland; somewhat less *Salmo stomachius*, the gillaroo of Ireland; but certainly not *Salmo carpio*, the trout of Lake Garda, Italy, with its whitefish-like shape and especially the large scales with a sharp delineation where the scales overlap. If unsealing the jars had not been a major project this would have been a good time to check the vomerine teeth.

Dr. Günther, of course, did not go by superficial appearance characteristics alone but checked a host of external and internal anatomical characters. With such a storehouse of information it is not hard to understand his difficulty in making classification judgments. Borrowing from the eloquence of Winston Churchill, the brown trout can be characterized "as a riddle wrapped in mystery inside an enigma."

In 1884, Francis Day,[18] in reviewing the Salmonidae of Great Britain, attempted to simplify the matter. Although Day described numerous population units of both brown trout and sea trout, he concluded they were all one species, *Salmo trutta*. In 1911, C. Tate Regan,[19] also a British authority, concurred with Day but went a step further in simplifying classification by grouping all British Isles and Continental strains of brown trout, which he, too, filed under *Salmo trutta*.

In 1932, L. S. Berg,[20] Russian authority on the zoogeography of the fishes of Eurasia, tried to finalize classification by combining all brown trout of the creature's original range into one species, *Salmo trutta*, but kept the taxonomic kettle simmering by dividing *Salmo trutta* into six subspecies: *Salmo trutta trutta* Linnaeus, the brown trout of northern and western Europe; *Salmo trutta labrax* Pallas of the Black Sea and tributaries; *Salmo trutta caspius* Kessler of the Caspian Sea and tributaries; *Salmo trutta macrostigma* Dumèril of the Mediterranean region; *Salmo trutta carpio* Linnaeus of Lake Garda, Italy; and *Salmo trutta aralensis* Berg of the Sea of Aral and the Oxus River.*

As Dr. Trewavas[21] of the British Museum (Natural History), now retired, points out, "The Linnaean system of binomial nomenclature is simple and the trout situation is complex."

Because of the complexities, the trinomial, or three-name, designation has long been accepted in taxonomic circles. When I was getting my fisheries training at Cornell, subspecies and the use of the trinomial were accorded new popularity. Students, too, were classified

---

*Berg does not reduplicate the name *trutta* for the typical subspecies but, following Dr. Trewavas, I do so to avoid confusion with the species.

either as "lumpers" or "splitters." Splitters were the grinds who spent countless hours in the laboratory going over field collections, checking fin rays, gill rakers, scales, vertebrae and other characters. Such dedicated drudgery was rewarded with the detection of all kinds of differences which, by self-supporting arguments, justified classifying the finny fellow as a subspecies.

Lumpers, following the lazy man's route, put all look-alikes in one taxonomic basket, using the binomial. It is no secret that by temperament and talent, I was a lumper.

In the case of the brown trout, the point has been reached where we lumpers have been vindicated. All the name-calling has come to an end. *Salmo trutta* as the scientific name of the brown trout is accepted by ichthyologists throughout its original and adopted range and has the stamp of approval of the International Commission on Zoological Nomenclature.

No longer does the brown trout have an identity problem, a problem which involved scientists and the geography of the world. On its own, *Salmo trutta* has won a special spot in the geography of the heart of the angler.

34

The Compleat Brown Trout

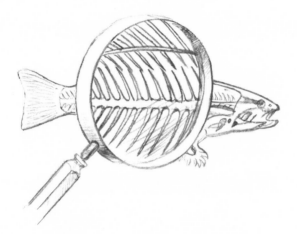

Anatomy: Inside

The brown trout, as we have seen, has an identity problem. The problem, however, is with the scientist and the fisherman, not the fish. *Salmo trutta*'s swashbuckling temperament does not lend to psychological hangups.

And the identity problem is mostly skin-deep. Under the skin lies an area with more uniformity. But,

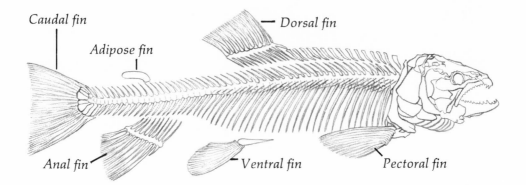

Caudal fin

Adipose fin

Dorsal fin

Anal fin

Ventral fin

Pectoral fin

The brown trout's caudal fin is firmly attached to the end of the backbone; the paired pectoral fins are joined to the shoulder girdle at the back of the skull; the paired ventral fins are fastened to bony plates embedded in the belly; the dorsal and adipose fins are not attached to the skeleton.

again, scientists, have discovered anatomical variations. As Aristotle noted over two thousand years ago: "We must not expect a degree of accuracy which is not inherent in the subject."

It might be expected, for example, that the number of vertebrae in a brown trout's backbone would be uniform and constant. Not so. Ichthyologists have discovered that in different parts of its range the number of backbone segments varies from fifty-eight to sixty-two. Whether this variation is due to heredity or environment was long a hot topic in the scientific community. Out of years of experiments and discussions has come the conclusion that the deviation is not an inherited character but due to environmental influences.

J. Schmidt[22] and A. V. Tåning,[23] working independently, demonstrated that water temperature at a certain period early in the development of brown trout influenced the number of backbone vertebrae.

It has been discovered, too, that the temperature of water in which trout are raised can also modify head and body proportions and other structural and functional characters.

Beneath the brown trout's exterior covering with its infinite pattern and color variations is a fairly standardized chassis. There is a skull, and a backbone whose first joint is rigid—the remaining joints are flexible, permitting easy and efficient body-bending in swimming. Ribs are located above the backbone and below, protecting the organs in the body cavity. On supporting ribs hang a series of W-shaped muscle segments adjoining and fitting into one another along the length of each side of the body. Nature used a fish in her first effort to create a face in the animal world. A fish, however, lacks facial muscles; consequently the fixed stare which may have inspired the coinage of the term "fish face."

The muscles are the part of the fish we eat. It is remarkable that such an active creature as the brown trout can have muscles so tender and succulent, such an epicure's delight. The brown's tail fin is firmly attached to the end of the backbone; the paired pectoral fins are joined to the shoulder girdle at the back of the skull. The other fins—dorsal and adipose—are not attached to the skeleton; the paired ventral fins are fastened to bony plates embedded in the belly.

The brown trout is a seventy-million-year-old model, yet it has the efficiency of a twentieth-century motor car. But the system which produces the brown trout's astonishing pizazz is not unlike the internal machinery of man. In the brown trout as in all animals, including man, it is the blood that ties together the system which keeps the trout going.

The engine that does the work is that big muscle, the heart. In the brown trout the heart is located just behind the mouth. In contrast to man's two-stroke system in which the blood goes from heart to lungs, then back to the heart to start its journey around the body, the brown trout has a one-stroke system: the heart pumps the blood to the gills, where it is purified and continues on its way to the vital organs, one stream taking the most purified blood to the brain while another stream goes to the other parts of the body. Valves at strategic points keep the blood circulating in one direction.

Scientists long ago discovered that the heartbeat of a fish varies with the water temperatures of its environment, increasing as water temperatures rise, decreasing as temperatures drop.

The heartbeat of a brown trout can be readily observed under a binocular microscope when the young fish is in the sac fry stage of development. I recall vividly my own first close-up look at the beating heart of a brown trout. Anton van Leeuwenhoek, inventor of the microscope, could not have been more thrilled when he turned the lens on living things for the first time in the seventeenth century.

Under the tutelage of Dr. Louis Wolf, I proudly clicked the microscope into a higher magnification, watching in rapt wonder the heart pumping blood to the vital organs in a steady rhythm.

During my visit to the New York State Fish Pathology Laboratory to check on the ability of brown trout to swim without fins, Neil Ehlinger and his staff made some heartbeat counts on brown trout under controlled water temperature conditions.

Counts were made on sac fry that had hatched

Plate I

THE AUTHOR'S FAVORITE DRY FLIES

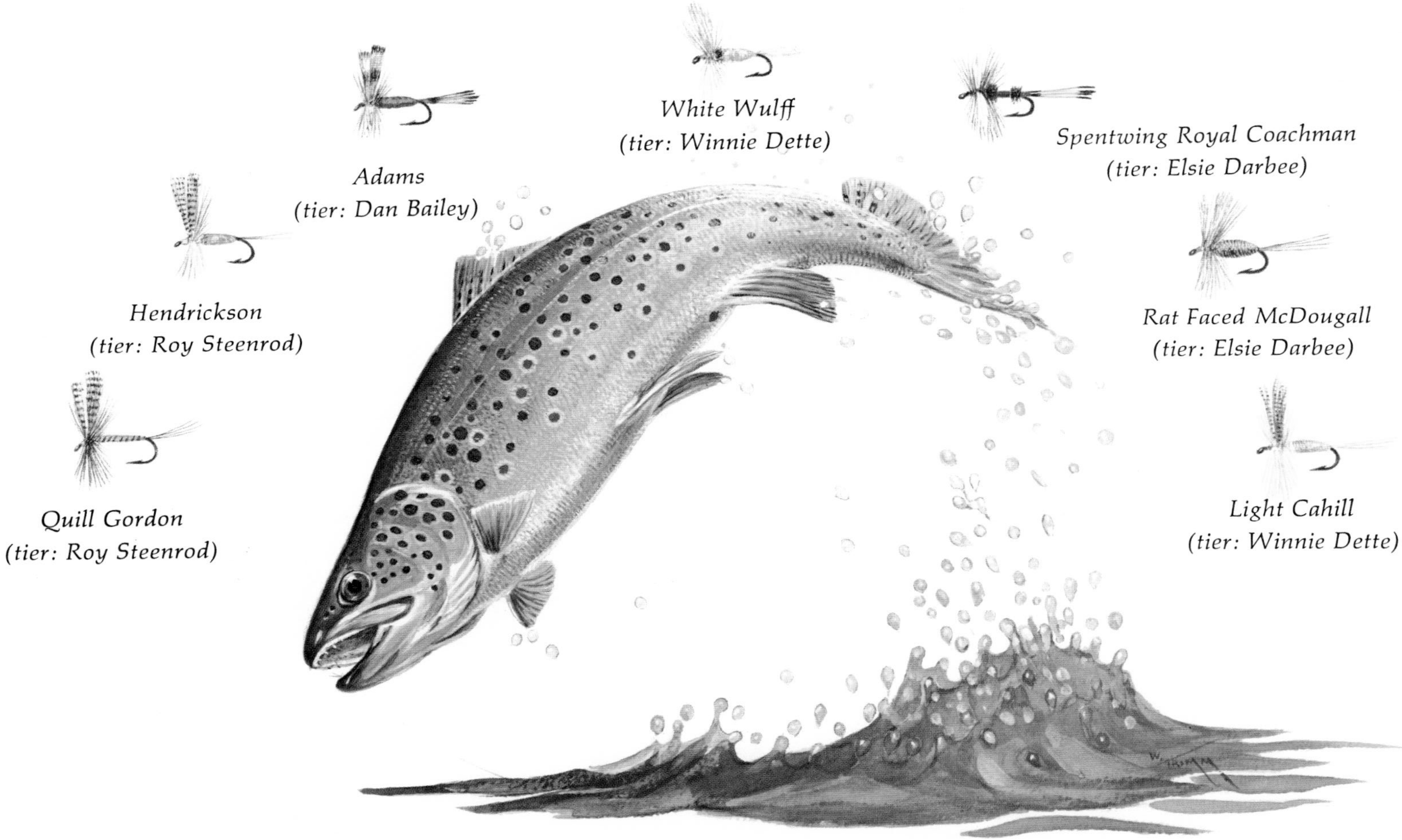

Spentwing Royal Coachman
(tier: Elsie Darbee)

Rat Faced McDougall
(tier: Elsie Darbee)

Light Cahill
(tier: Winnie Dette)

White Wulff
(tier: Winnie Dette)

Adams
(tier: Dan Bailey)

Hendrickson
(tier: Roy Steenrod)

Quill Gordon
(tier: Roy Steenrod)

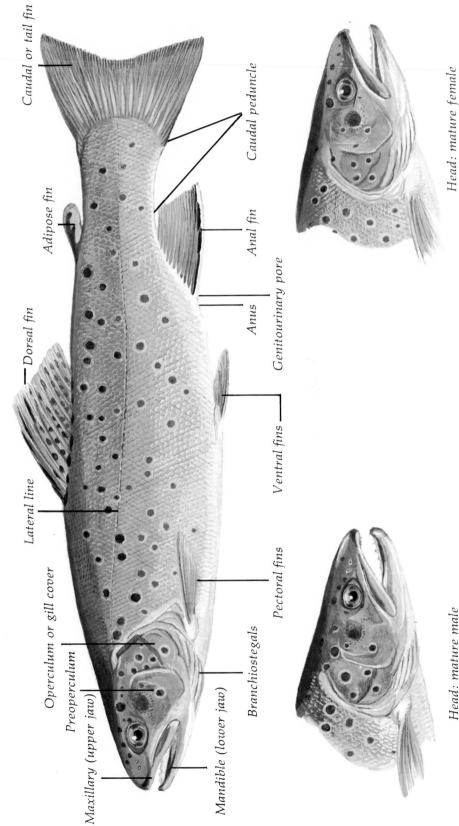

Plate II

EXTERNAL ANATOMY OF THE BROWN TROUT

(From brown trout caught by author)

Caudal or tail fin

Caudal peduncle

Adipose fin

Anal fin

Dorsal fin

Genitourinary pore

Anus

Lateral line

Ventral fins

Operculum or gill cover

Preoperculum

Pectoral fins

Maxillary (upper jaw)

Branchiostegals

Mandible (lower jaw)

Head: mature female

Head: mature male

Plate III

INTERNAL ANATOMY OF THE BROWN TROUT

(From brown trout caught by author)

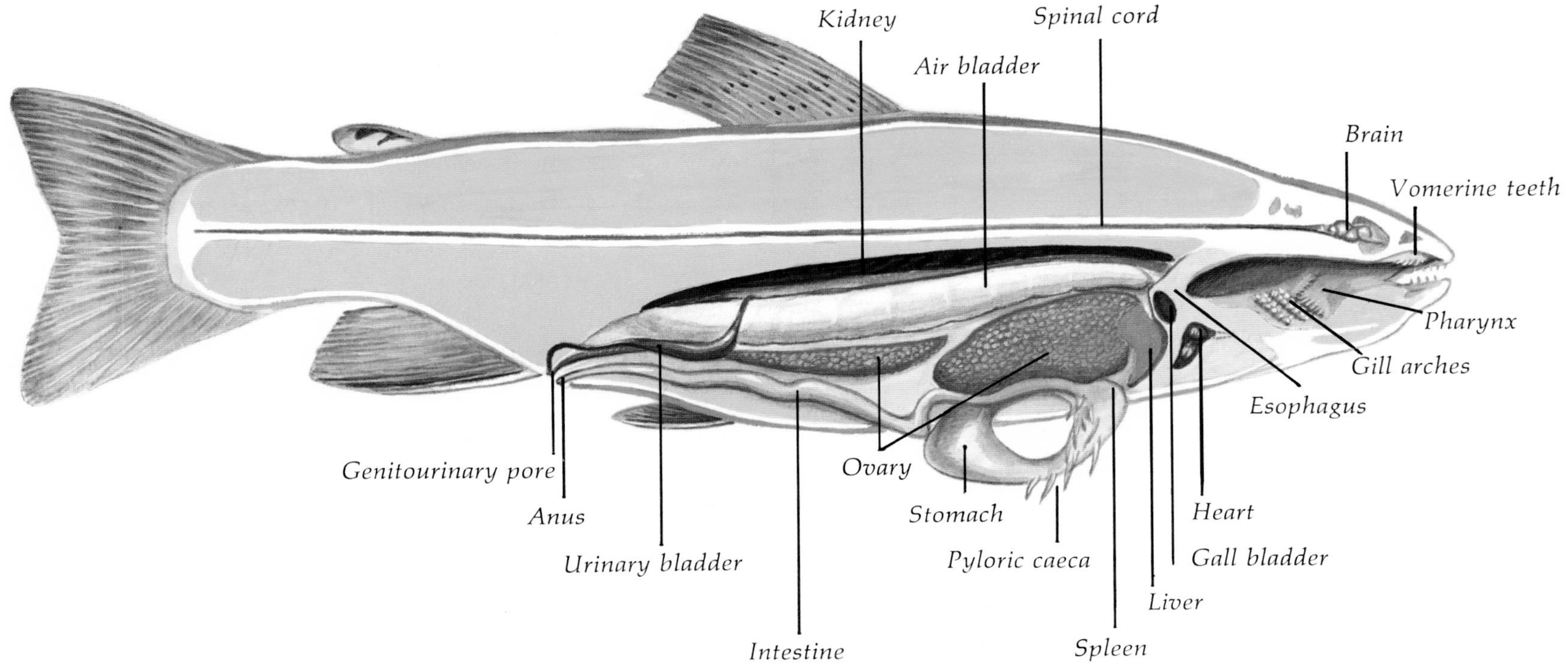

Vomerine teeth

Pharynx

Gill arches

Brain

Esophagus

Heart

Gall bladder

Liver

Spleen

Spinal cord

Pyloric caeca

Air bladder

Stomach

Kidney

Ovary

Intestine

Urinary bladder

Genitourinary pore

Anus

Plate IV

GROWTH PROCESS OF THE BROWN TROUT

Advanced fry—fingerling

Yearling

Eyed egg

Sac fry

Mature brown trout

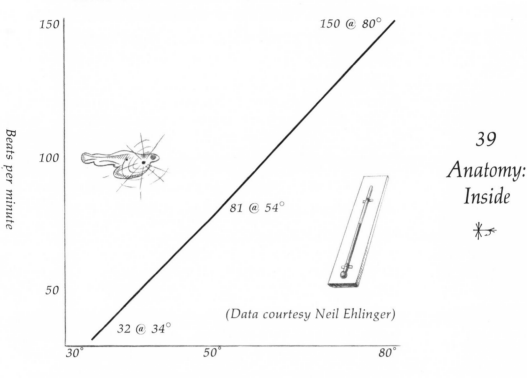

HOW TEMPERATURE
AFFECTS THE BROWN TROUT'S HEARTBEAT

Beats per minute

150

150 @ 80°

100

81 @ 54°

50

32 @ 34°

(Data courtesy Neil Ehlinger)

30°   50°   80°

from twelve hours to one week before. At normal hatchery water temperature, 54° F., the heartbeat was 81 strokes per minute. When temperature was lowered to 34° F., the heartbeat quickly dropped to 32 beats a minute; when temperature was elevated to 80 degrees, the rate accelerated to 150 beats per minute.

The hardiness and adaptability of *Salmo trutta,* even at this early stage, showed up when the sac fry were removed from 80° F. water and put in 54° F. hatchery water, and the heartbeat returned to a normal 81 beats per minute. At the end of four days' observation, the tiny fry revealed no ill effects.

Oxygen in the blood keeps the living machine activated. For the brown trout, as other fishes, water is the source of oxygen. To obtain oxygen from water, nature has provided gills which take the place of lungs. There are four pairs located in a chamber just under the gill cover on each cheek of the trout. A gill consists of a bony arch to which are attached blood-red filaments full of blood vessels. As water leaves the trout's mouth, it passes through openings between the gill arches, permitting the filaments to absorb oxygen and release the blood's waste products, chiefly carbon dioxide.

When the trout's mouth opens, water is sucked in as the gill covers close; when the mouth closes the floor of the mouth, acting as a pump, rises and forces water past the gills as the gill covers open. The respiration rate is normally about fifty openings/closings a minute, the rate increasing under stress or an increase in water temperature.

Water often contains bits of debris which might injure the delicate gill filaments. Again nature has provided protection. The gill arches are equipped with straining devices called gill rakers.

Although no one has observed the brown trout's internal anatomy in action, many processes are enough like man's to make logical comparisons.

The digestive system of the brown trout begins at the mouth, which is ideally designed for capturing food, with teeth on the upper and lower jaws, on the roof of the mouth and even on the tongue. At the end of the throat is the esophagus, leading to the stomach. The throat is equipped with a protective device, a pharynx, a constriction which opens only when food is passing into the stomach, preventing the stomach from being constantly flooded with water.

Following the esophagus in the digestive train is the U-shaped stomach and the intestine with an opening, the anus, for the disposal of wastes.

40
The Compleat Brown Trout

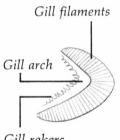

Gill filaments

Gill arch

Gill rakers
(20 or fewer
on first gill arch)

INTERNAL ANATOMY OF THE BROWN TROUT

(see also Color Plate III)
(From brown trout caught by author)

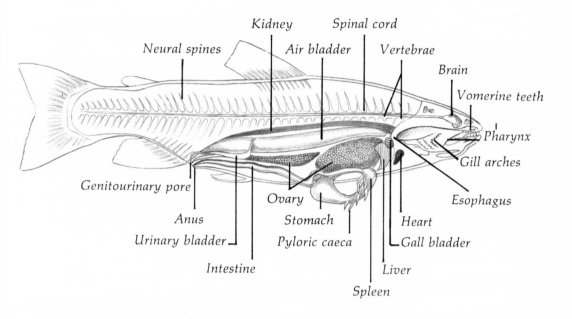

Attached to the posterior end of the stomach are pyloric caeca, not found in the vertebrate world above the class Pisces. The twenty or so fingers of the pyloric caeca, grayish or white, are sometimes mistaken by anglers for tapeworm. The function of the caeca, it is generally believed, is to retain food for slower digestion and a more efficient utilization of food.

Unlike man, brown trout do not have sluggish periods. *Salmo trutta* is always fueled up and ready to go. Although a brown may often be seen resting in the backsets out of the current, it is always on the alert for a choice morsel which may pass nearby.

The body tissues of such an active animal as the brown trout undergo constant wear and tear. In the digestive process, proteins, fats and carbohydrates break down into amino and fatty acids, glycerol and sugars.

Products absorbed by the cells in the intestinal wall pass into the capillaries, where they are picked up by the blood. Undigested food continues through the intestine to the anus and is discharged.

In the process of replacing worn-out cells, the digestive process also produces toxic waste products such as ammonia, eliminated through the gills, along with carbon dioxide. Some liquid wastes and excess water are voided through the kidney—a dark-red organ, located under the backbone, which opens into the genitourinary pore just back of the anus.

Lying under the kidney is the brown trout's air bladder. A fisherman dressing a trout seldom recognizes this flat, glistening membrane as the air bladder because it is invariably deflated when a trout is being cleaned.

In ichthyological circles, few subjects open up the floodgates of controversy more than the function of a fish's air bladder. It has been considered a hearing aid, as in cod; a means of communication, as in weakfish; an auxiliary oxygen tank for emergencies; a warning gauge to keep fish from getting the bends; and a hydrostatic balancer.

The brown trout's body is compressible, expanding or contracting with changes in water pressure. If a brown trout is not to be in a continuous struggle with its environment, its body should have the same weight-to-volume ratio as the surrounding water. When it rises to the surface to snatch a mayfly or darts to the bottom to escape an enemy it must be able to maintain this equilibrium. Regulating the air in the air bladder enables it to do this.

Most of the tissues in a brown trout's body are heavier than water, so the trout will have a tendency to sink. Again, by varying the amount of air in the air bladder, the trout can maintain a position at practically any depth, often almost motionless, fins barely moving.

When *Salmo trutta* travels from a freshwater habitat to the ocean, the air bladder is indispensable. A brown trout in hydrostatic equilibrium in fresh water will tend to float in heavier salt water. The contraction of the trout's air bladder reduces its volume and brings weight-to-volume ratio in line with the specific gravity of sea water. When as a sea trout *Salmo trutta* returns to fresh water, it will tend to sink until the air bladder is expanded and again the weight-to-volume ratio of the trout's body matches that of fresh water.

Despite many studies by qualified scientists, some of the functions of the air bladder of a brown trout are incompletely or sometimes imperfectly understood. Indeed, several of the other physiological processes must be viewed as theoretical, hypothetical and still unproved.

Even so, what we know about the inner workings of the brown trout gives us a better understanding of this great sporting fish—a fish with rugged endurance, a stout heart and a fighting spirit.

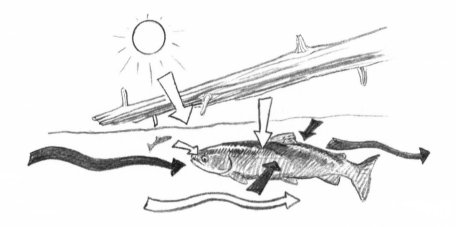

Senses

Every fly fisherman who has ever spooked a brown trout after a most careful approach knows the fish has keen eyesight. But can *Salmo trutta* smell or detect different odors? Taste or distinguish flavors? Feel pain? Hear sounds as human beings do? These questions have intrigued fishermen and scientists for centuries.

Once when grouse hunting I stood on a bridge watching a brown trout in the pool below. The brown was practically motionless, gills and fins working slowly. Out of curiosity I fired my 20-gauge in the air. There was no visible reaction. Then I waved my arm, casting a shadow on the water. Immediately the trout scooted for the nearest hidey-hole.

Fishermen have learned they can talk loudly at streamside or in a boat without scaring trout. But the footfall of a booted foot or the banging of an oar on the side of the boat sends them scurrying for shelter.

Sounds to brown trout are apparently vibrations in the water. Aerial sounds, which humans hear readily, do not seem to penetrate the water enough to register with trout, unless, as in a blasting detonation, the sounds are accompanied by vibrations traveling through the ground to the water.

The brown trout does not have external ears. Nothing like our crude appendage, a sort of funnel to catch sounds. Nor does it have a middle ear. A trout does have internal ears—a pair entirely inside the skull.

A brown trout's internal ears may pick up some vibrations and help it detect sounds, but evidence indicates that the ears are less related to hearing and more associated with balance. The brown trout's ears contain semicircular canals, not unlike those in the human ear, which with their sense organs enable it to be aware at all times of its position in the water. This equilibrating device keeps the trout upright and swimming straight even in the complete darkness of deep muddy water.

Scientific consensus considers the brown trout's ear a minor organ for hearing. That mysterious organ, the lateral line canal, performs the chief functions of hearing.

The lateral line is found only in animals dwelling

in water. On the brown trout the lateral line is plainly visible on both sides of the body from the tail to the edge of the gill opening. The line also extends across the gill cover to the head. Often embedded in the skin, the line is frequently invisible in this area.

The lateral line consists of a tube or canal under the skin, filled with mucus and opening into tiny holes on a horizontal line of scales along the midsection of the body—the visual effect to an observer being like the Plimsoll line on a ship. Under the canal are sense organs connecting to the spinal cord or main nerve trunk, which leads to the brain.

As a hearing organ the lateral line in the brown trout works like this: Vibrations in the water, such as the footfall of a boot, push against the fluid in the lateral line canal; the resulting pressure stimulates the sense organs under the canal, which send signals to the brain via the nerve trunk.

This marvelous sonarlike device can pick up vibrations of very low frequency. Another fish swimming nearby is readily detected and avoided. Waves reflecting back to a moving trout from sunken logs and submerged rocks are picked up by this echo sounder, helping to keep the trout from bumping into obstacles.

Recent experiments indicate that the lateral line may also act as an aid in recognizing thermal conditions, warning a trout when there are sudden introductions of heated water into a stream, as from a powerplant, or low-level releases of cold water from a reservoir.

The sense of touch is the most fundamental of all senses in animals, even in the lowest forms of life. Remember looking at the one-celled paramecium through a microscope in school days? The little fellow darts away at the slightest touch.

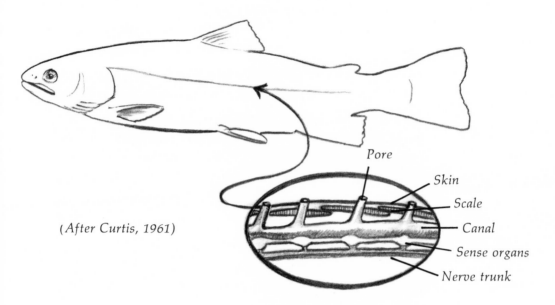

Pore

Skin

Scale

Canal

Sense organs

Nerve trunk

(After Curtis, 1961)

The lateral line consists of a tube or canal, filled with mucus, running along each side just under the skin. Opening to the outside through a series of muciferous pores, it appears as a slightly raised line between the tail and the gill cover. This line of perforations, sometimes embedded and invisible, extends across the gill cover and ends in a shotgun pattern in back of the eye.

Beneath the canal, a nerve trunk runs parallel to the canal, sending out branches at intervals. Each branch is equipped with sensory endings or ampullae.

Vibrations in the water, even of a very low frequency, cause the viscous fluid in the canal to move and stimulate the sense organs which send appropriate messages to the brain. Reflection of vibrations back to the trout enables the fish to "hear" the presence of a nearby fish or obstacle.

The sense organs of the brown trout are spread over the surface of the skin. Thus, a trout usually starts squirming at the slightest touch. Anglers know so well there's many a slip between unhooking a trout and getting it in the creel.

Yet, in taking spawn, hatchery workers, with skilled and knowing hands, can calm the most unruly trout. Poachers, plying their profession, depend on the "tummy tickling" technique—a trick of the trade in capturing trout hiding under boulders or undercut banks.

In spite of being so sensitive to touch, it is doubtful if a trout feels pain as a human feels pain. A classic case history is the timeworn story of the ice fisherman who caught a trout, foul-hooked in the eye. The trout was released and the eye used for bait. Soon the tip-up flag waved. The one-eyed trout had been hooked again.

Fly fishermen are familiar with the experience of releasing a small trout, then resting the pool because the little fellow thrashed around so wildly, only to have the released trout take the fly again, sometimes on the first cast.

Can a brown trout smell? "Yes," the bait fisherman answers promptly: "I've often noticed when I take off a waterlogged worm and put on a fresh one I get a strike."

"That's because the fresh worm was wriggling and attracted attention," claims the skeptic.

"But salmon or trout eggs—the fresher the better—are the best bait of all," counters the fisherman. "And eggs certainly don't wiggle."

Scientific investigations indicate the sense of smell in brown trout is well developed and they probably can distinguish certain odors.

In brown trout the receptors of smell, like man's, are located in the nostrils. The trout has twin nostrils on each side of its head—tiny holes in the top of the snout. They do not connect with the throat as in the human nasal system but open into blind sacs just under the skin. The sacs are lined with sensory tissue, and cilia, or tiny moving hairs, keep water moving into the front nostril and flowing out the rear nostril.

Some fisheries workers are convinced that the sense of smell is so strong in sea trout that on migration they are able to recognize the odor characteristic of their home stream.

Taste, like smell, is a sense which responds to a chemical stimulus. The inside of a brown trout's mouth is generously supplied with taste buds, but it has not been determined how highly developed the taste sense of brown trout is.

For instance, is a brown's palate so educated that it can distinguish between a male and female mayfly? Art Flick, for example, found that brown trout are sometimes so selective they will feed exclusively on Red Quills (males) or Hendricksons (females) even when both sexes are hatching at the same time.

Is such finickiness purely taste? Or smell? Or a combination of the two senses? Is there an attractive metallic taste, like oysters, associated with spinning

Nostrils.
Water enters front opening,
flows out rear opening.

lures? How do nocturnal feeding browns find their food?

Here is an area of investigation which opens up a real can of worms.

Of what are popularly known as the five senses—sight, hearing, touch, taste and smell—the brown trout's sense of sight heads the list, a basic equipment in its survival kit, helping *Salmo trutta* to capture food and avoid enemies.

Dry-fly fishermen are invariably impressed with a brown trout's keen vision, judgment of distance and ability to be on target: the fly is moving, the trout is moving, and the water is moving, yet when a brown trout is on the feed in earnest, it seldom misses. Anatomists point out the unusually large optic lobes in the brain of the brown; they are about the size of the cerebellum, the part of the brain which controls movement.

Long ago, an angling writer, observing the similarity between the eye of a trout and the eye of man, concluded that a trout saw objects the same as man. This is one of those half-truths which become as firmly embedded in angling literature as a hook in a trout's jaw.

The outer surface of the brown trout's eye is flattened and streamlined in keeping with its slim shape, offering minimum resistance to the water. The brown's eye consists of an eyeball filled with vitreous humor, a transparent jellylike substance; a cornea which serves as a protective covering, also transparent; an iris, a ring of silvery olive green with a hole or pupil, permitting light rays to enter; a lens, which bends the incoming rays to form an image; a sensitive retina, composed of rods and cones, on which the image is formed; and an optic nerve connecting the retina with the optic lobes in the brain.

The brown trout's optic system, like the human op-

EYE OF MAN

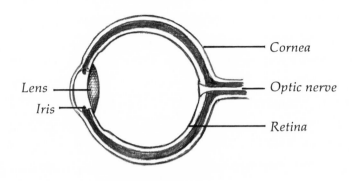

(After Curtis, 1961)

EYE OF BROWN TROUT

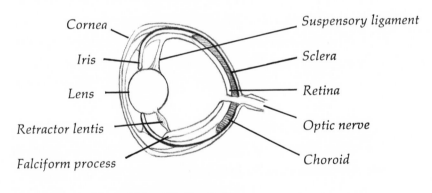

(After Walls, 1942)

tic system, has been compared with a camera's operation: a lens, iris, retractor lentis (focus adjuster) and retina (sensitive film).

There are, however, several significant differences between the eye of the brown trout and the eye of man.

First, the trout has no eyelids. In man, the eyelids, a

sort of windshield wiper, keep the eyes moist and clean. In its watery element, a brown trout has no need for eyelids.

Another distinguishing difference is the shape of the lens. Spherical in shape, like a glass marble, the lens of the brown trout is designed to permit light rays entering water to form clear images. In contrast, the lens of man's eye is elliptical, better for registering images of light rays entering through air.

Another marked difference is the functioning of the iris. In the brown trout, it cannot be enlarged or reduced in size like the iris in man, which provides protection from bright sunlight. Since the amount of light entering water is slight, the trout gets along fine with a fixed iris opening.

Moreover, the trout has a unique muscle, the retractor lentis, a focusing device which permits the entire lens to be moved toward or away from the retina as long-range or short-range vision is needed.

The eyes of a brown trout are located on opposite sides of the head, and each has a specific field of vision. However, straight ahead beyond the nose, the right and left eyes combine in a common, binocular field.

A trout's vision is acute, of course, in its natural medium, water, but it also sees objects well through the air. Occasionally, in false casting close to the water, I've had a brown trout leap clear of the water in an attempt to capture the passing fly.

With a background of high-school physics, I'm not about to cross pens with experts in the field of optics. And even the experts disagree on some points. As Josh Billings, local crackerbarrel philosopher at the turn of the century, noted: "It's better not to know so much than to know so much that ain't so."

Yet, even at the high-school physics level, the sub-

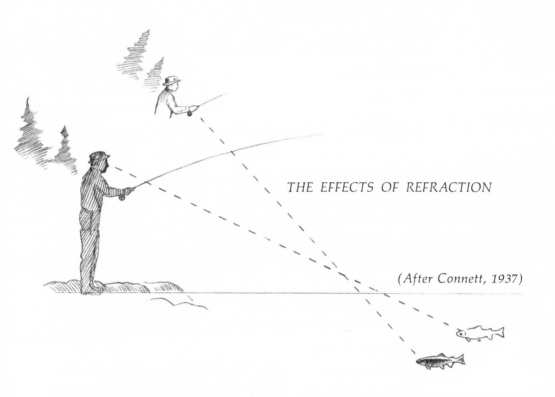

THE EFFECTS OF REFRACTION

(After Connett, 1937)

ject offers helpful hints to the angler. Especially that basic principle that a ray of light passing from air to a denser medium like water is refracted or bent.

On those rare occasions when a trout is spotted up ahead, it will help an angler to recognize that because of the laws of refraction the trout is not at the location it appears to be. Remember the classroom demonstration—a ruler dipped into a basin of water seems to bend upward? Because of the same phenomenon, the trout appears to be closer to the water's surface and slightly ahead of its real position. On long floats, such a situation offers no problems, but in tricky currents and in tight casting, it should be remembered that a fly dropped over the spot the trout appears to be to the fisherman's eye will actually be above the fish and will float down through pay-dirt territory.

For fishing success, however, it is more important to know how the trout views the angler than how the

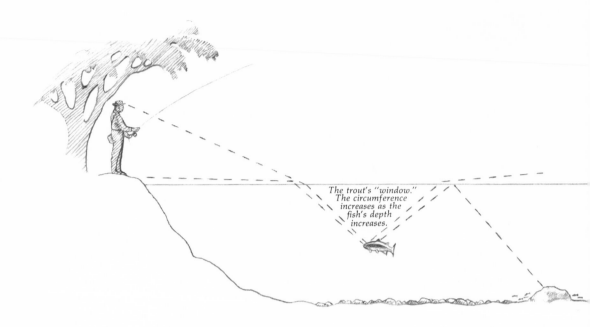

The trout's "window." The circumference increases as the fish's depth increases.

angler views the trout. In fact, because of the laws of refraction, the trout sees the angler much more often than the angler sees the trout.

When a brown trout looks upward from its watery world, vision is confined to a cone-shaped area with an angle of about 97 degrees. Long known by anglers as the "trout's window," it has a skylight-like circular opening at the water's surface. The size of the opening varies with the depth of the trout below the surface. At a depth of 3 feet, the circumference of the opening is a little over 6 feet. The nearer the surface, the less a trout can see. At 6 inches below the surface—where brown trout often feed during the peak of the dry-fly fishing season—the window is only 6 inches in diameter. Ruffled water cuts down on what a trout sees through the window, one reason why broken pocket water pays off so well.

Outside the circumference of the cone is an opaque area which acts as a sort of mirror, reflecting back into the cone of vision objects off the bottom.

Early in the game, George La Branche was aware of this aspect of a trout's vision and gives good advice on fishing the floating fly over a trout hiding under a rock or sunken log. "To reach a fish in this position," he suggested, "or rather to place the fly so it will be seen by him, an imaginary circle should be drawn about the spot . . . and the fly fished on this curved line until the circumference has been covered."

Many anglers, I think, have been led to believe that the trout's vision is limited to the view from the 97-degree angle of its window. Again, the lessons of high-school physics are recalled. Refracted light rays put objects on the bank of a stream within the visual field of a trout up to a distance of about 20 yards.

Dr. Frank W. Law,[24] an English observer, in refining some details regarding a trout's vision through the window, warns: "It is true if we crouch or creep to the bank, we present a smaller object and thus stand a better chance of being unobserved; but never let it be thought that at any time we can see the fish while he cannot see us. The laws of optics prohibit this."

I'm puzzled when I see a dry-fly fisherman tie a No. 20 fly on a 7X leader, crawl on his belly to get within casting distance of a glassy pool and then wave his rod high in the air in false casting. Experienced anglers keep the rod as near the horizontal as possible.

How about the dry-fly man's perennial question: "Can a brown trout distinguish colors?"

Gordon L. Walls[25] in his in-depth study of the vertebrate eye stated: "The reader's suspense, if any, may as well be relieved at once by the flat, if somewhat backhanded statement that no fish is known *not* to have color vision."

Experiments on fish in laboratories with colored foods have demonstrated that many species display a preference for certain colors. But I refuse to believe these laboratory tests apply to dry flies of different hues fished in the field under various levels of light intensity.

Like other members of the dry-fly clan, I like to believe that a brown trout can distinguish not only colors but different shades of a color. Theodore Gordon once remarked that if he ever found out trout were color-blind all the fun would go out of fishing. He tied his Quill Gordon in three mutations, each dressed in a different shade of hackle. Gordon recalled an occasion when a continuously rising brown refused numerous tries with the first two versions but took the third translation on the first cast.

If a trout's eye sees objects like the human eye, a fly of almost any color will appear merely as a tinted silhouette against a blue sky; against a backdrop of dark-green foliage, the tints will be more pronounced.

Perhaps the effectiveness of a hair-wing fly is a better penetration of light between the hairs, which throw off a spectrum of tantalizing light rays irresistible to the most recalcitrant brown.

I live in apprehension that a scientist will subject my favorite dry flies to spectrum analysis, which will take away their lure for me if not for the trout.

Even a brief look into the sensory equipment of the brown trout puts scientists and anglers hip-deep in theory and conjecture. Moreover the brown trout, in addition to a full complement of conventional senses, has a "sixth sense"—an uncanny sense of survival which makes it the most difficult of all the trouts to catch.

Tropisms

Many anglers scorn book learning but, looking back on six decades of fishing, I am increasingly aware of my debt to formal, professional training.

Successful brown trout fishing is a study in animal behavior. With brown trout as with other animals, behavior is closely associated with the senses we have just been discussing. Here we lean heavily on the academic world.

When I was at Cornell, Dr. George C. Embody opened new doors for me which not only added to my knowledge but increased my compulsive attraction to angling in general and devotion to the brown trout in particular.

The Professor and I, although of different vintages, had an unusual teacher/student relationship. Coming from the same hometown in central New York State, we shared a bond which extended beyond a love of trout fishing to an affinity for Scotch whisky.

I still remember his lecture on trout tropisms which helped me apply a fruitful, new approach to my quest for the brown trout.

Tropism is the tendency of a plant or animal to turn toward or away from a source of physical stimulation such as light, heat and contact. We are all familiar with the phenomenon of a sunflower turning its head to the sun. A brown trout's reaction to light also governs its behavior pattern. Thus, a brown trout is said to be phototropic. Because *Salmo trutta* shuns light and prefers dark places, it is negatively phototropic.

Early in my salad days in conservation, I learned

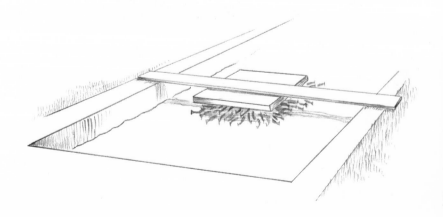

about a very practical application of phototropism. Shortly after starting work in a trout hatchery I was assigned to an old-timer to help him sort and grade to size a trough of brown trout fingerlings. Brown trout, like children, do not grow uniformly, and the bigger trout often make a meal of the smaller trout. To keep cannibalism from putting a dent in production, trout are sorted and size groups separated.

I watched Old Charlie set up for the job. Fresh from the classroom, I proudly announced, "You know, you're taking advantage of the trout's phototropic proclivities."

"You college fellers," he snorted. "I'm doing no such thing. I've been takin' care of this batch since they was hatched and they're doin' fine."

But, unknowingly, hatchery men for years have been relying on phototropism to do their sorting for them. A slatted divider is placed in a hatchery trough. Half the trough is covered to shut out light. Trout put in the uncovered section immediately try to get into the dark, covered area. The small trout get through, but not the larger trout. By varying the space between the slats in the divider, trout can be separated into fairly uniform sizes rapidly and with very little handling.

Anglers also instinctively put phototropisms to work. It does not take a fly fisherman long to learn that as light intensity fades, brown trout come out of their hiding places seeking food in open riffs and pools. The "evening rise" is not just a nice bit of poetic imagery but is based on a sound principle—the phototropic response of trout.

Anglers are also applying a practical use of phototropism when, during daylight hours, they seek their quarry under boulders, sunken logs and undercut banks. Sometimes overhanging brush provides enough of a shaded area to harbor a trout or two even under a bright sun. And on those nights that are black as an espresso, the meat fisherman goes after big browns in the large economy size.

"Only the game fish swims upstream," wrote John Trotwood Moore. The poet's description fits perfectly the brown trout. This reaction to a stream's current is known technically as rheotropism. Heading upstream, the brown trout is classified as negatively rheotropic compared to a fish like the bullhead which drifts downstream with the current. This is an advantage to the angler: the brown's negatively rheotropic reaction to stream currents keeps the fish facing upstream, reducing the trout's view of the angler who approaches from the rear.

Currents, and especially eddies, can be deceiving. Eddies often put reverse English on a current. One of my most satisfying fishing recollections was the time I decoded a tricky current on the Tenmile River, near my Dutchess County, New York, home. Dropping a Hen-

drickson below the spot I wanted to reach, I watched it move upstream in a half-circle to be smacked a moment later by a plump ten-inch brown. When I outwit a brown trout, I attribute success to my streammanship; when the trout outwits me, it's just hard luck.

A good time to study stream currents is when stream levels are low. The brown trout has a strong territorial imperative. Low water levels reveal a brown's favorite lies—sunken logs, boulders and bottom contours. A brown trout's favorite lie in low water is usually a favorite lie in high water, I've found.

Rheotropism in the brown trout helps make it the exciting fish it is. Walton noted the brown's affinity for currents over three centuries ago: "As he grows stronger, he gets from dead still water into sharper streams . . . he gets him in swifter and swifter streams and there lies at the watch for flie or minnow . . . and these make the trout bold and lusty."

Anglers know the brown trout as a free-swimming creature, avoiding direct contact with other objects, animate and inanimate, in its environment. Because *Salmo trutta* shuns touch, scientists characterize the brown trout as negatively thigmotropic. This response is the direct opposite of the brown's habitat associate, the sculpin or muddler, a small fish seldom seen by fishermen because it hugs the bottom of the stream.

Even when a brown trout's favorite territory is under a boulder, the trout touches neither the boulder nor the bottom. Thus a brown is always poised for action— either to avoid enemies or to make those lightning-fast forays for food.

As a dry-fly man, I suppose it is *lèse majesté* to pass on a trick of nymph fishermen who find bouncing a Wooly Worm along a stream's bottom, sweeping through pockets under boulders, a deadly effective technique.

The chemotropic reactions of brown trout are not only a concern of fisheries biologists but also open up opportunities for fishermen to add to their repertoire.

Brown trout are especially sensitive to the chemical composition of the water they live in. In a world of ever-increasing industrial growth, fish kills are commonplace. Lethal chemicals in factory wastes have caused the death of countless thousands of fish. But sometimes the natural environment itself develops problems associated with the chemotropic responses of brown trout.

During summer heat waves, for instance, when streams get low and sluggish, the slow-moving sections occasionally develop an oxygen deficiency. Brown trout seek the waterfalls for a rejuvenating oxygen cocktail, and knowing anglers concentrate on the spills and cascades where the action is.

Of all the tropisms, the brown trout's reaction to water temperature—thermotropism—ties in most closely with angling strategy.

During the Tom Collins season, browns gather in spring holes to ride out a heat wave. So smart fishermen also seek the spring holes. To the brown trout, the difference between a water temperature of 79° F. and 82° F. is vitally significant. To the trout that mere three degrees may be a life-or-death situation. To the fisherman it makes the difference between a feeding trout and a could-not-care-less trout.

Brown trout show a remarkable ability to adjust to a wide range of water temperature changes, provided the change is gradual, as in seasonal variations. During the coldest part of the winter when most streams are covered with ice, brown trout, although quite inactive, are comfortable in a water temperature of 33° F.

When the water warms up in the spring and summer, brown trout thrive until water temperatures reach 75° F. Laboratory tests have shown that browns can endure 81° F. temperatures for limited periods of time. But a stream running a temperature of 81° F. for any length of time is not a trout stream worthy of the name.

Sudden changes in water temperatures, however, are lethal, whether hot or cold. Fishermen have long known that discharges of heated water from industrial plants produce thermal shock to trout, but only recently have they become aware that sudden cold-water discharges such as low-level releases from reservoirs have equally disastrous effects.

Sometimes a brown trout is confronted by two or more tropisms which govern its responses. It helps an angler plan his strategy to know which tropism is dominant at the time. *Salmo trutta*, continually revealing its Arctic heritage, is a cold-water animal. Thus, thermotropism is stronger than rheotropism. A brown will leave a favorite position in a current to seek cooler water even if there is no perceptible flow, as in a quiet backset where spring water is seeping in from the bottom of the stream.

Thermotropism is also stronger than phototropism. During a heat wave, a brown trout will leave its usual dark hideout to live temporarily in an open section such as an unshaded spring hole or the outlet of a cold feeder stream.

And thermotropism is stronger than chemotropism. The urge to seek cooler water sometimes throws the brown trout a chemical curve. Spring holes occasionally contain an excess of nitrogen, sometimes causing trout to contract popeye disease—a symptom of too much nitrogen.

Brown trout are so responsive to thermal conditions that anglers should not downgrade water temperature as a guide to more successful fishing. Many fishermen scorn a thermometer. But, to me, a thermometer, like a rod or reel, is an essential piece of fishing equipment. However, like a woodsman's compass, it must be used properly. Just dunking a thermometer in the water willy-nilly is of little value and very often is confusing.

The time to start using a thermometer is when trout streams get low and the summer doldrums are beginning. An obvious spot to take temperatures is at the mouth of a tributary. To give more meaning to the reading, temperatures should also be taken in the tributary itself and a few yards above and below its confluence with the main stream. Sometimes the water in these small tributaries is warmer than that in the main stream.

Springs frequently seep in from the bottom and are undetected. Sometimes a little wildcatting pays off, especially on streams one has fished regularly so that a good working knowledge of thermal conditions has built up. On days when it is practically impossible to raise a trout yet suddenly a brown smacks the fly, it is wise to explore the spot. Occasionally the thermometer reveals an unexpected spring hole. In a lifetime of fishing I have discovered only two spring holes by wildcatting. But during the dog days of August, these two spots put me several percentage points ahead on the trout tote board, season after season.

In fishing for brown trout, the mind is often as important as the rod, line and lure. Smart anglers have learned that an understanding and interpretation of tropisms invariably beats blind, lock-step casting, helping to keep those fish-less days from coming up too often.

Salmo trutta's responses to light, water temperature, stream current and other physical stimuli demonstrate, too, what a wonderfully complicated and fascinating creature the brown trout is.

65
Tropisms

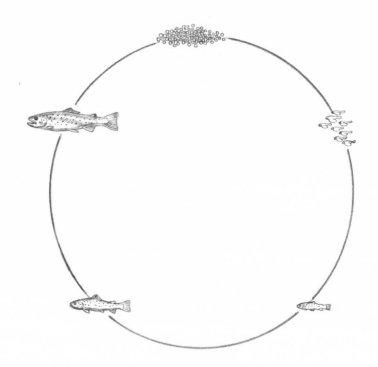

Life Style

Many Octobers ago, a grouse-hunting trip took me to the Crystal Creek area, a Grade A brown trout stream on the western flank of New York State's Adirondack Mountains, a stream where several years before I had worked on a creel census project.

As I rounded a bend in the stream, my eye caught

the golden flash of a brown trout flipping its tail in the gravel of a riff. As the silt cleared, I spotted another trout moving in alongside the first.

"Spawning," I said to myself, as I watched a repeat performance. At last, I was viewing with my own eyes the courtship of my favorite fish.

Fisheries biologists are natural piscatorial peeping Toms. To us voyeurs, the lovelife of *Salmo trutta* kindles much the same interest as an evening rise on the Beaver Kill in June. As a practicing journeyman of the trade, it had been a longstanding professional ambition to observe honeymooning brown trout.

Later, I proudly related my observation to Dr. John R. Greeley,[26] who, as Chief Aquatic Biologist, was my boss at the time in the New York State Conservation Department. A few years previously John, a pioneer fisheries biologist in America, had recorded the spawning habits of trout in the Pere Marquette, Manistee and other Michigan river systems. His report is still a classic in fisheries literature.

Looking down from his nearly seven feet with a characteristic wry side glance, John asked a few penetrating questions:

"Did you see any kind of a mating clasp?"

"No."

"Did you see a cloud of milt and perhaps a few eggs rolling around?"

"No, but I did see a lot of silt being stirred up."

"I have a feeling," John said quietly, "you were watching the preliminaries—the nest building—not the main event."

The courtship of the brown trout takes place in the fall of the North Temperate Zone, from September through December, but usually in October and November. The remarkable adaptability of *Salmo trutta* shows up even in its lovelife. Below the equator, in the South Temperate Zone, brown trout adjust to the fall season of the Antipodes—April, May and June.

In the Kenya highlands, a mile or so high and smack on the equator, there is no autumn. The sex instinct of the brown works overtime. Individuals in a population unit turn to thoughts of love at different times and spawning occurs throughout the year.

For the United States' brown trout populations Dr. George Embody had a neat capsule summary: "The brown trout spawns in the fall on rising water, falling temperatures and diminishing light intensity."

In modern fish culture, the control of light intensity in hatchery ponds is adjusted so spawning time is telescoped. Eggs can be taken in August and September—a boon to hatchery workers who have long suffered frozen fingers taking spawn in October and November.

New facts are continually being uncovered about the brown trout's sex life. For instance, Dr. W. E. Frost and Dr. M. E. Brown[27] suggest that the pituitary gland, located under the brain, may also be significant in spawning since this "master gland" produces several hormones which affect the endocrine tissue in the sex organs, which, in turn, influence spawning behavior.

Several months before courting time, sex changes are taking place inside the body of the trout.

In the male brown trout, the testes appear first as two fine white threads situated just below the air bladder. As spawning time approaches, the white threads turn creamy pink and begin to swell as they fill with milt, containing the spermatozoa. The testes narrow at the posterior end and join in one tubelike duct which empties into the genitourinary pore.

The ovaries of the female brown trout are also situated under the air bladder, in the same relative position

as the testes, and like the testes they run lengthwise inside the body cavity.

The female brown's ovaries are always recognizable as saclike organs containing tiny beadlike swell-
ings. The sac, a thin, transparent, almost invisible membrane, contains the maturing eggs. The eggs are not
loose in the body cavity as some of the early scientific
fishing literature recorded—a belief fostered because in
dressing a trout around spawning time, it is almost impossible to avoid slitting the delicate membrane so the
eggs spill out into the body cavity.

During their development stage a few eggs in the
membrane collapse and disintegrate. Some authorities
believe this breakdown results in a chemical reaction
which produces hormones necessary for successful egg
development.

As the brown trout undergoes physiological
changes associated with its amorous activities, a geneti-
cal phenomenon is also taking place. The nucleus of
every living cell in the body contains a specific number
of chromosomes. The number for *Salmo trutta* is eighty.
Each egg receives half this number from the female and
half from the male, contributed during the spawning act
when the egg is fertilized by spermatozoa—tiny wigglers
which under a microscope look like a cluster of
commas.

Whether appearance, growth rate and age of sexual
maturity are due to heredity or environment or a combination invariably opens up the floodgates of controversy among scientists.

In trout hatcheries where a major objective is the
large-scale production of fast-growing, early-maturing
stock, selective breeding techniques seem to throw the
balance on the side of heredity. In the wild, where governing conditions vary not only from stream to stream

but in different sections of the same stream, environment appears to be the dominating influence.

The lovelife of the brown trout in the wild is one of nature's most intriguing stories. In thirty years of professional observation, I've noticed it's the first heavy rains of fall—the "line storms"—which turn the brown trout's fancy to thoughts of love. The stream in spate creates an attractor current which starts *Salmo trutta* upstream on the annual spawning migration.

The female swims on ahead to select a suitable site for the nest or redd. Like many a newlywed, some are pretty choosy, others not so fastidious. A perfectionist bride moves upstream slowly, nosing here and there, carefully checking currents and intently on the lookout for a combination of gravel sizes necessary for a satisfactory nest. Very often the site finally selected is in a riff above the swiftest water at the tail of a pool. Here, currents readily percolate through the gravel to ensure a silt-free, well-aerated area of sufficient size to accommodate several individual nests at one spawning site.

After the site has been selected, the female awaits the arrival of a male, resplendent in brilliant breeding colors, and then begins to dig a pit in the gravel. With precision that designers of modern excavating machinery would envy, she turns on one side, ventral fins spread to anchor her body for leverage, cutting the gravel with vertical sweeps of her powerful tail. Clouds of silt rising punctuate the process. Now and then she moves away but returns, using her anal fin to test depth and contours.

The female does all the work in preparing the nuptial bed. It is the male who has selected the female as his mate—perhaps with her consent. He does not help with the digging or cutting but remains close by, usually a few feet to the rear.

Occasionally—more frequently as actual spawning time approaches—he moves in by her side, snuggling up romantically and quivering a little.

Sometimes another male—often a precocious yearling, stimulated by such piscine passion—comes out of nowhere, trying to muscle in on the snuggling act. The older male, the hook on its lower jaw giving it a menacing mien, moves in quickly to drive the intruder away. The rival—or rivals, for sometimes there is more than one—keeps returning and is driven away time after time. However, if the intruding male is larger, the new Lothario steals the bride.

During the period just before spawning, the female also helps in defending the nest, protecting it on the upstream side while the male acts as a rear guard.

After an hour or more of digging, the female has created a pit about 6 inches deep and 12 inches in diameter. Satisfied with the nest and completely wooed, she stops digging. Intent on consummating the marriage, she remains on the nest, pectoral and ventral fins well spread for a firm holding position. Her mate now moves in alongside. Heeled over like a sailboat in a stiff breeze,

his position puts his vent close to hers at the deepest point of the pit.

There is a tremendous quivering of arched bodies. As the quivering reaches a crescendo, eggs and milt are released at the same time, clouding the scene until the current clears the water.

Sometimes at the moment of orgasm, a small yearling, barely at the age of puberty, rushes in. Stimulated and quivering with uncontrollable desire, the young buck trout ejaculates his pent-up milt. Such an act confuses the paternity of the offspring, and the rightful male is like a bridegroom being cuckolded in his own bed on the first night of the honeymoon.

A honeymoon that is just beginning. With vigorous flips of the tail, the female buries the eggs in the nest to a depth of 8 to 12 inches with a protective hummock above. She then moves upstream a few feet and starts digging another nest, where the mating game is repeated. And again. And again. Finally all of the eggs have been extruded and the female is "spent" and finished with spawning for the season. As for her mate, all during the nuptial ceremonies he has not only shown an ability to fight off rivals but has demonstrated that he is quite a swordsman, too. So much so that he now deserts the nest and goes off in search of another female interested in romance. The spent female remains at the nest for several hours, putting the finishing touches on a protective covering of gravel over the eggs—a covering not only to protect against invaders but to permit a percolating flow of water through the gravel. When finished, the original hummock disappears and the nest is indistinguishable from the adjoining stream bottom. At the end of the operation, the eggs are from 4 to 6 inches below the top of the gravel.

Now the female leaves the nest. From this time on a brown trout is an orphan.

The eggs now begin a long incubation period, varying with water temperature. In the Beaver Kill and other Catskill rivers where anchor ice is part of the streamscape during the long winters, water temperatures hang around 33° to 34° F. for several months. In this low temperature, brown trout eggs may require five months or more to hatch.

About the middle of the incubation period the egg reaches the "eyed" stage, so named because a jumbo-sized eye shows clearly through the egg envelope.

Shortly before hatching the embryo begins to

EGG TO PARR

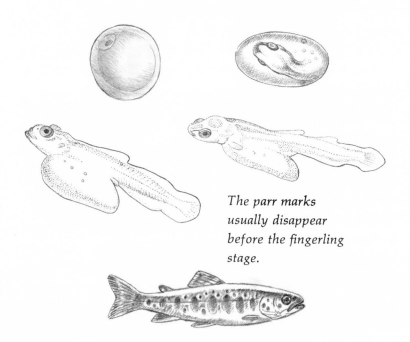

The parr marks usually disappear before the fingerling stage.

squirm around inside the egg. With spasmodic kicking movements at intervals the tiny creature finally breaks out of the egg. Rupturing the egg releases an enzyme which helps to dissolve the egg envelope. Brown trout eggs, although fertilized practically at the same time, do not hatch at the same time. The time spread may extend over several hours or even a day or more.

When the newly hatched brown trout kicks out of its egg, the little fellow has a globular yolk sac—a portable lunch box—attached to its belly. The sac contains the remains of the egg yolk, providing high protein nourishment.

By the time the yolk sac is absorbed, the little fellow's mouth and fins have developed so it is free-swimming, able to forage for food on its own. It now resembles its elders in shape and structure. To a trained eye, the little critter is recognizable as a brown trout.

As with wines, vintage spawning years occur now and then—seasons when conditions for a bumper spawning are exactly right, tasting for the angler taking place three or four years later.

Growth rates of *Salmo trutta* vary in different climates. Growth in lakes differs from growth in streams: lake browns generally grow faster, live longer and attain a larger maximum size.

When a stream brown is one year old, its length ranges from 3½ to 5½ inches. At the next birthday, it will be from 5 to 8 inches. By the middle of the fishing season in its third year, a brown trout, under average conditions, is a satisfactory size for sport and food. In the golden age of the Beaver Kill, a three-year-old 12-inch brown trout, weighing one pound, was a hallmark of the stream.

The age of a brown trout can be determined by examining a scale. A brown trout scale has a lot to tell—almost a complete autobiography. "Fish life on a small scale," Dr. John Greeley characterized it.

A brown trout's scale looks not unlike a man's fingerprint, with rings, called circuli. The circuli resemble the growth rings of a tree, except the rings are added continuously as the trout grows and not each year.

Salmo trutta is born naked; scales begin to form when a fry is slightly over an inch in length, growing in practically the same proportion as the trout grows in length.

The growth rings are narrowly spaced in slow-growing trout, more widely spaced in faster-growing trout. When there is a cessation or slow-down in growth, as during the winter, the interlude is reflected in the scale structure—a formation called a "winter band." This winter band or annulus is used to calculate the age of a trout.

During the spawning period the drain on a brown trout, especially the female, slows down metabolism so much that a portion of the outer edge of the scale may actually erode away before the trout resumes normal growth.

Thus a practiced eye assisted by a microscope can tell not only the age of a trout at the time of capture by counting the annuli but, by back-calculation, its size at the end of each year of its life; if the trout has spawned and the number of times. For a sea-run brown the time spent in a stream and the time it resided in the ocean can be estimated with reasonable accuracy. It is even possible to recognize a scale that has replaced one which has been knocked off. In my halcyon days as a practicing fisheries biologist, scale reading was one of the most fascinating of the many fascinating chores that went with the job.

The brown trout is a relatively short-lived animal.

Average life expectancy is a mere three years. Early life mortality figures would rock the most blasé actuarial expert.

In the wild, the survival of brown trout eggs to the fry stage is surprisingly high, a hatch often equal to survival in hatcheries. But then comes a crash decline. From fry through fingerling stage, a loss of over 90 percent takes place. Both yearlings and two-year-olds suffer a 50-percent loss each season. If a brown trout's nest originally contains a thousand eggs or so, only three or four individuals will survive to their fourth year.

Despite these devastating statistics, *Salmo trutta* maintains stable populations in countless streams throughout the world year after year, demonstrating the brown's extraordinary instinct for survival.

Male brown trout normally become sexually mature at the end of the second year. There are a few adolescents whose maturity is delayed another year and, as

BROWN TROUT SCALE

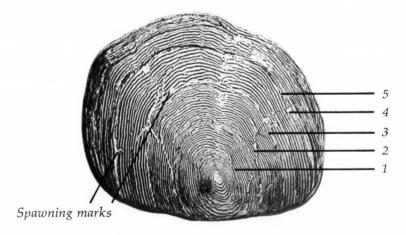

Spawning marks

(*Photomicrograph and data courtesy Dr. U. B. Stone*)

CALCULATING AGE
AND GROWTH FROM SCALE ANNULI

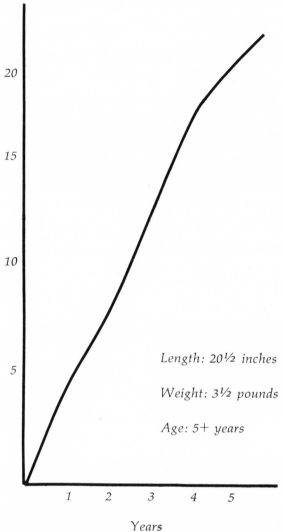

Length: 20½ inches

Weight: 3½ pounds

Age: 5+ years

Formula (Fraser, 1915):

$$L^1 = C + \frac{S^1}{S}(L - C)$$

L = length of trout when scale sample taken
L^1 = length of trout at given annulus
C = length of trout at time of scale formation
S = length of entire scale radius
S^1 = length of scale radius to given annulus

Calculated lengths

Annulus	Length (inches)
1	4.2
2	7.7
3	12.4
4	17.1
5	19.5

we have noted, some precocious young buck yearlings who rush in on a spawning couple at the height of love-making.

Most female browns mature in the third year. Here, too, are precocious individuals and some with sexual hangups which postpone maturity. But, normally, in the third autumn of her life, a female brown trout will start nosing her way upstream, methodically testing gravel, currents and other components of a nest, finally finding a site to her liking. A site where another generation of brown trout is in the making and another round of fishing pleasure is beginning.

On the Production Line

My first conservation job was in a trout hatchery where I acted as a baby sitter for several million brown trout. Situated on a curve of the Mohawk River at Rome, New York, the hatchery's rearing ponds had been converted from a spur of the historic Erie Canal—a section whose fame was recorded by Walter Edmonds in *Rome Haul* and *Drums Along the Mohawk*.

Rome was strictly a production hatchery and did not use up valuable space by holding brood stock. As a fifth-wheel neophyte I was often put out on loan to Caledonia, Saranac and other sister hatcheries in the New York State chain where breeders were held. A break for me; it helped to round out my hatchery education.

The marvel of the brown trout in nature has been matched by the miracle of creating brown trout through artificial fish culture.

Artificial reproduction has not only helped to maintain populations of brown trout in the streams and lakes of its original range but has also made it possible to introduce the great game fish into new waters in every part of the world.

At the knee of seasoned experts I learned some of the basics of trout culture. Like taking spawn.

I watched these hatchery veterans strip trout with a skill that made the operation look unbelievably easy. Scorning the canvas glove on the left hand, so much in use today, they held a big female trout barehanded just above the tail fin while the right hand pressed gently against the belly and released a golden stream of eggs into a basin held by another worker. Quickly, using the same belly-pressing technique, generous squirts of milt—containing the spermatozoa—from a male or two were mixed with the eggs, fertilizing them immediately.

As a greenhorn, I was permitted merely to hold the basin. But one day Old Charlie, whose experience dated back fifty years, to the earliest days of fish culture in America, spoke up:

"Son, you gotta learn to strip some time." He pointed to a plump 3-pound female brown trout. "Try that one, she's good and ripe."

The trout immediately recognized an untrained

hand as I tried to pick her up. She protested. She squirmed. She got away. Flopping on the ground, eggs began spilling out of her vent. I was speechless with dismay and humiliation.

"Try again," was Old Charlie's only comment.

The next try I did better. At least I was able to hold on to the trout, and it was so ripe, eggs flowed out at the slightest touch.

The way Old Charlie stripped trout is still standard operating procedure in trout hatcheries everywhere.

And has been for over five hundred years. Dom Pinchon, a French monk, first described the method in 1420. His experiments took place near the Abbey of Rheôme at Montbard in the Côte d'Or, the renowned Burgundy region of France. After the females and males were stripped, he placed the impregnated eggs in a gravel-bottomed trough of running water for incubation. Naturally, the monk used brown trout for his experiments, the only trout native to the region and part of *Salmo trutta*'s original range.

Dom Pinchon's vintage manuscript, written before printing, did not turn up for several centuries. It came into the hands of the Marquis de Montgaudy, a grand nephew of George Louis Leclerc, Comte de Buffon, naturalist to Louis XV and, at court, a favorite of Madame de Pompadour.

The Marquis de Montgaudy revealed the work of Dom Pinchon at a meeting of the Société Zoologique d'acclimation de Paris early in the eighteenth century.

Early in the same century, a Prussian army officer, Stephen Ludwig Jacobi, began experimenting with the artificial reproduction of brown trout at his Westphalia estate, using methods much like Dom Pinchon's. Jacobi published the results of his thirty years' experiments in 1763, and, for a while, was hailed as the originator of fish culture, an accomplishment considered so important that the British government granted him a pension.

Still later, in 1842, two unschooled French fishermen, Joseph Remy and Antoine Gehin, rediscovered the methods of Pinchon and Jacobi. The work of Remy and Gehin came to the notice of Professor M. Coste, teacher of biology at the College of France. Professor Coste, who later wrote the first book on fish culture, advised the Académie Française. The Académie persuaded the French government to establish a hatchery, the world's first trout hatchery. The facility was established at Huninque in Alsace-Lorraine just across the Rhine from Basel, Switzerland. I always regretted not making a pilgrimage to the world's first brown trout hatchery when I was in Basel a few years ago.

All these early experiments, of course, were with *Salmo trutta,* because it was the only trout available. In the United States, the first experimenters worked with the brook trout, native to eastern North America.

The first efforts took place in 1853 when Dr. Theodatus Garlick and Professor H. S. Ackley stripped brook trout captured in Michigan's Au Sable River and transported the eggs to Ackley's farm near Cleveland, Ohio, where they were incubated in a makeshift hatching trough.

In 1859, at West Bloomfield, New York, Stephen Ainsworth, a friend of Dr. Garlick's, made the first attempt in this country to establish artificial trout propagation on a production basis. Ainsworth captured wild trout, permitted them to spawn naturally in troughs, retrieved the fertilized eggs and placed them on trays in troughs of running water for incubation.

Ainsworth did not fully succeed in making fish culture a financial success. The man who did was Seth Green. Green was both a dreamer and a doer. A native of Rochester, New York, he made frequent visits to nearby West Bloomfield to observe Ainsworth's operations. Soon Seth Green spawned ideas of his own, setting up a hatchery at Caledonia, New York, in 1864. In a few years, Green's plant proved a profitable commercial venture. His layout design of hatchery troughs and nursery ponds became a model for dozens of hatcheries which soon began to spring up all over the United States and Canada.

Seth Green, with a touch of modern Madison Avenue in his personality, far outshone his contemporaries, earning him the title "Father of Fish Culture in America."

Green's hatchery was taken over by New York State in 1868. Green remained as foreman for several years, also serving on the New York State Fish Commission.

When the brown trout was introduced to this country, the Caledonia hatchery included the species in its propagation program. The newcomer, however, was thoroughly disliked, especially by fishermen who had established reputations earned with impressive catches of native brook trout. They found the brown a much tougher adversary. And their images tarnished. Moreover, self-styled gourmets complained about the eating qualities of the brown compared to native trout.

In 1964, the hundredth anniversary of the founding of the first fish hatchery in America was celebrated at Caledonia. It was my pleasant chore to represent the New York State Conservation Department at the event.

A testimonial luncheon honoring the occasion was held at Spring Brook Inn adjoining the hatchery grounds, a hostelry dating back to Seth Green days. Here Theodore Roosevelt was entertained during an inspection trip when he was governor of New York.

Roosevelt, a keen sportsman and qualified naturalist in his own right, was also a stickler for native American species. At Spring Brook Inn he was served trout but not told it was brown trout until after the meal.

"Bully," replied T. R. with his characteristic vigor. "It's equal to the best trout I ever ate."

Roosevelt's reaction marked a turning point in brown trout history in its adopted land. Opposition to the foreigner began to wane. With the arrival of dry-fly fishing, *Salmo trutta* firmly demonstrated its virtue and value as one of the greatest of the freshwater game fishes.

Among those at the anniversary luncheon was Harry Annin. His father, James, had built a trout hatchery just above Green's site, and Harry operated it for fifty years. Harry, another early mentor of mine, knew Seth Green as an immense stocky man with a beard of patriarchal proportions.

"When I was a boy," recalled Harry, "our elders told us a mouse lived in that great beard. All of us kids in the village were always looking for chances to be around Seth, hoping to get a glimpse of the famous mouse—a hope, I'm sorry to say, that was never realized."

In my own hatchery days, the work was much the same as in the time of Seth Green. After stripping, the eggs were placed on trays in troughs of running water. My most vivid memories are the seemingly endless days bending over a hatchery trough picking out "ringers." Ringers are dead eggs, readily recognized by their chalk-white appearance. Working against time, we tried to remove the dead eggs before fungus formed and infected the adjoining healthy eggs. Eggs are picked up either with a suction bulb or forceps. I was brought up on forceps, made of wood. Each tong was equipped with a

84
The Compleat
Brown Trout

wire ring just the size—one-fifth of an inch—to grasp a brown trout egg, and at the other end of the forceps was a turkey feather to gently brush the live eggs aside.

The egg-picking chore lasts nearly two months. In New York and other states in the northeastern United States, most trout hatcheries use springs as a water supply. Water temperatures will run around 50° F. both in the winter at incubation time and later during the spring and summer rearing period. Hatcheries have a rule of thumb: at a constant water temperature of 50° F., brown trout eggs will hatch in fifty days.

When newly stripped brown trout eggs are put on trays in running water, they expand to their maximum size and quickly become what to the trade is known as "water-hardened." These "green eggs" are hardy for

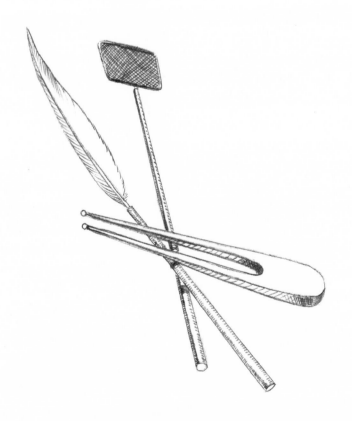

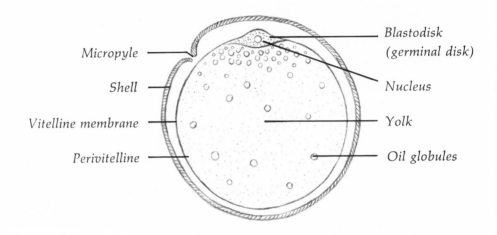

Micropyle

Shell

Vitelline membrane

Perivitelline

Blastodisk
(germinal disk)

Nucleus

Yolk

Oil globules

(After Embody, 1936)

about forty-eight hours, able to withstand considerable handling. Hatcheries use this period to transport eggs. Otherwise they become tender and must be held until the "eyed stage" when they become hardy again.

One day I was standing next to Old Charlie on the egg-picking routine and he said: "You know one time we had another college feller here that was even more stupid than you."

Old Charlie, a self-made fish culturist, was a no-nonsense, straight-from-the-shoulder guy. Continuing, he said: "A big shipment of brown trout eggs was comin' in from our Randolph Hatchery . . . missed connections at Westfield . . . got put on a slow train that got delayed in a snowstorm . . . when the train finally pulled into Rome, the eggs was gettin' near the tender stage . . . we worked most of the night settin' 'em on the trays . . .

the next day was Sunday when we always have a lot of people rubberneckin' . . . most of 'em with kids runnin' around like crazy . . . the young college feller heard the boss say, 'I hope the visitors don't bump into the troughs' . . . our young feller went up to the workshop and made up some signs—'Please Don't Jar the Troughs'—and started to tack 'em up on the troughs. The boss caught him before he got too far . . . told him his hammerin' was doing more jarrin' than a busload of visitors . . . I'll tell you, he was a pretty sheep-faced feller for a couple of days."

The care and feeding of brown trout is an around-the-clock, seven-day-a-week job.

After the fry have hatched, the yolk sac—that portable lunch box—has been absorbed and fins and mouth have formed, the free-swimming fry develop a glutton's appetite. In my fish hatchery days, to speed up growth, the little fellows were actually trained to feed by dipping a turkey feather in a liver paste and trailing the feather in the water up and down the length of the trough.

A few days later, the turkey-feather technique was replaced by the dipper routine. The liver mixture was placed in a long-handled dipper, perforated on the bottom. Shaking the dipper vigorously released tiny particles of the mixture. The fry soon fed with gusto, some rising to the surface to catch tidbits. A heartwarming sight to any dry-fly fisherman visualizing hooking one of these surface feeders a couple of years later. But now I found that instead of suffering from "egg-pickers' back," I developed a "fish-feeders' wrist"—akin to a tennis elbow.

With rising food costs, the pure-meat diet which Seth Green started would bankrupt any hatchery in the country. Today, pellets scientifically compounded with all the necessary ingredients, and in various sizes, do the job.

In a month or so, the fry are transferred from the hatching troughs inside the hatchery to outside nursery troughs. Here the fry soon grow into fingerlings and are put into large rearing ponds.

New York State trout hatcheries were the first to use scientific feeding formulae. Pioneers like Tunison, Haskell and Deuel[28] helped fish culture keep pace with the science of nutrition already developed in other fields of animal husbandry.

This new breed of college-trained fish culturists developed a hatchery feeding chart now used in most of the trout hatcheries in the United States. For example, the amount of food fed to a batch of hatchery trout is correlated with their total body weight. With this procedure it is possible to determine the number of pounds of food required to produce a pound of trout; thus a "conversion factor" is established providing an index for the efficiency of the diet.

Indeed, modern nutrition knowledge enables hatchery diets to be as carefully measured as a baby's formula. In fact, the Deuels put these findings to work, recording the progress of their baby son, David. Tacked up in the kitchen, a standard hatchery feeding chart was used to keep a record of food fed the baby, and his conversion factor was determined. As a testimonial to the hatchery chart, David not only survived but thrived, eventually following his father in fisheries work.

Besides the never-ending nuts-and-bolts chores, hatchery workers are sometimes confronted with critical life-and-death situations, as when disease strikes.

In the wild, the brown trout is an unusually healthy animal. Although a healthy trout is sometimes a carrier—Furunculosis Freddy instead of Typhoid Mary. But in hatcheries where several million fish are kept in close confinement, a disease outbreak is a constant threat. Under crowded mass-production conditions, disease assumes epidemic proportions, sweeping through the entire population of a hatchery.

Brown trout, like people, can get all kinds of ailments. Some are similar to human diseases—goiter, caused, as in humans, by an iodine deficiency; or eye cataracts; or fatty degeneration of the liver. Brown trout also get ulcers, ugly raw sores on the body caused by bacterial infection. Also bacterial in nature are furunculosis and fin rot.

DISEASES OF BROWN TROUT

*Fin rot
(can affect any fin;
formerly considered
a specific disease,
now part of a syndrome
of many disorders)*

External parasites

Ichthyophthirius   *Trichodina*   Gyrodactylus

*...s bubble disease
...fects blood vessels
...fins; caused by
...ersaturation
nitrogen
oxygen*

*Cataract
(characterized by
opacity of lens,
as in human beings)*

*Gill disease
(cause not fully
worked out; accounts
for heaviest mortalities
in hatcheries)*

Internal parasites

*Furunculosis
(most common bacterial
disease of brown trout;
infection starts inside
and progresses outward
but is often not visible)*

*Goiter
(caused by iodine
deficiency in water)*

*Ulcer
(rare in brown trout;
infection starts outside
and progresses inward)*

*...oundworms
...ematodes)*

*Tapeworms
(cestodes)*

*Flukes
(trematodes)*

The most common afflictions of brown trout, however, are not noticeable. They are caused by diminutive
external parasites, of which there are dozens of species,
all requiring a microscope for identification. The most
common external parasitic affliction of brown trout is
ichthyophthirius—a bugaboo known to all hatchery
workers as "the itch."

One time, at his fish-pathology laboratory on the
grounds of the Rome Hatchery, Dr. Louis E. Wolf
showed some of us hatchery workers slides of the
critters.

One fellow worker looking up from the microscope remarked: "Now I know where necktie designers
get their ideas for those wild ties."

When I mention giving trout a bath, people think
I'm putting them on. Yet one of the most effective treatments for parasitic infections is a simple salt bath: the
infected trout are put in a hatchery trough and the flow
of water is shut off for a short time. Quickly salt is distributed throughout the trough in the proper percentage. When the water is turned on again, the trout are
noticeably improved, although several treatments are
sometimes required for a complete cure.

Various up-to-date chemicals and drugs are also
used as disease-control agents, such as Terramycin and
sulphamerazine.

When I was at Cornell, a few of Dr. George Embody's more imaginative students rigged up what they
called the "disease eradicator": a big holding tank for
ailing fish where chemical solutions could be measured
and regulated by control valves. On a few occasions,
there were some unfortunate mishaps. Disasters, in fact.
The "disease eradicator" was rechristened the "fish
eradicator."

With its characteristic hardiness, vim and vigor, the

brown trout makes an ideal fish for artificial reproduction. Although brown trout may be domesticated, they do not remain tame for long after they have been transferred to a natural habitat, soon developing a full complement of wiles and a satanic cunning which continues to baffle the most expert angler.

91
On the
Production
Line

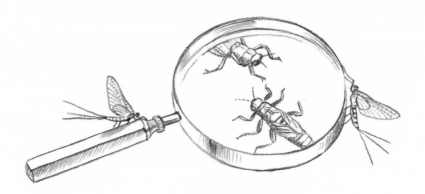

Food

The favorite food of the brown trout—mayflies—makes *Salmo trutta* the favorite quarry of the dry-fly fisherman.

But the brown trout, by nature a carnivorous creature, can be caught on a host of critters which wiggle or swim, crawl, jump or fly. Stomach analyses show that, at times, *Salmo trutta* feeds on plankton, worms, slugs, scuds, ants, bugs, beetles, bees, wasps, flies, grasshoppers, crayfish, salamanders and fishes, including an occasional brother or sister.

The brown trout can also be lured by a variety of inanimate hardware. I recall a couple of seasons ago on the Tenmile River when a local farmboy, armed with a spinning rod and phoebe lure, snaked a plump 10-inch brown right out from under my Hendrickson, floating perfectly through a long, narrow pool.

I was chagrined, not with the boy but with myself. How could such a hard-to-catch fish as a brown trout become such easy prey? Before the boy arrived I had, with what I modestly believed to be adequate finesse, blitzed the pool with a dozen casts without stirring up one bit of interest.

During the Depression of the 1930s, I worked in the kitchen of the Lake Placid Club, deep in the heart of New York's Adirondacks. In that gray period of America's economic history it was a good job, providing three meals a day—and one of the best brown trout streams in America at the doorstep, the West Branch of the Ausable River.

One of the chefs, an Adirondack native, had acquired a reputation in the North Country for taking big brown trout in the West Branch—attested to by the magnificent specimens in the kitchen's ice chest.

How he did it, no one knew. And the chef wasn't telling. Then, one day, I discovered his secret weapon. I caught a glimpse of him, late for duty, rushing in with a fish and hurrying to the ice chest before grabbing his toque blanche and taking his station at a range.

Always envious of his prowess, I peeked in the chest for a look at his latest conquest. There on a bed of ice was a noble 18-inch brown. But fastened under the big hooked jaw was a jointed pikie minnow plug. The big fish had been foul-hooked—caught in a crossfire of two gangs of treble hooks, a sort of piscatorial acupuncture.

To a devout dry-fly angler, the chef's method, although highly successful, is *lèse majesté*. As one of the dry-fly clan, I don't quarrel with a fisherman's right to use any legal method. I just feel a little sorry for an angler who does not know the joys of fishing the dry fly.

The brown trout's affinity for a natural floating fly—almost always a mayfly—makes dry-fly angling the most fascinating, most satisfying of the trout-fishing options. To those anglers who have been hooked on the romance of the brown trout/dry-fly marriage, there are few pursuits in life to equal the witchery of watching a well-directed dry fly complete its appointed task. If these thoughts strike no responsive chords then no amount of explaining will explain them. It is akin to a wine sophisticate trying to explain the subtle distinctions between a Burgundy and a Bordeaux to a confirmed Dr. Pepper drinker.

I was a very young Catskill fisherman when I caught my first brown trout. At that time the common earthworm was the only kind of bait I knew. For carrying garden hackle, a prized possession was a little tin box with a hinged lid, crescent-shaped with belt slots to fit around the waist, enameled in forest green with the glowing word *Leurre* stamped in gold on the front of the box.

In those days, I had no idea trout could be caught on flies. I thought the swarms of flies I noticed hovering over Rondout Creek were moths and butterflies.

One day, eavesdropping around the crackerbarrel at Ben West's General Store in Napanoch Village, I caught snatches of talk about a new kind of fishing—fishing with flies. I was so naive that I actually thought the men were talking about houseflies and wondered how they fastened them on the hook. I was puzzled until, shortly after, Mr. West stocked an assortment of wet flies on gut-snelled hooks.

Too shy to ask questions, I studied long and intently the flies in the case on the counter spread out next to Rocky Ford cigars and Copenhagen snuff. My allowance went for the gaudiest, of course. Mr. West's flies did not catch trout, but they caught me.

Years later, at Cornell University, I was exposed to basic training in entomology, which served to deepen my interest in fly fishing.

Still later, by a great stroke of good fortune, the Catskills of New York became part of my beat as a fisheries biologist. I found a spin-off benefit of the job was the opportunity to fish the Beaver Kill, Willowemoc, Neversink, Delaware, Esopus, Schoharie and my beloved boyhood stream, the Rondout.

By this time I knew the "moths" with their tentlike wings, lying thick as snowflakes on the rhododendron, were caddis flies and the "butterflies" hovering over the stream in yo-yo fashion were mayflies.

Mayflies have come to mean nearly as much to me as the brown trout. These days, it seems, I spend much of the year waiting for the mayfly season to arrive. The old bromide about the impatience of youth is a mere fribble compared to the impatience of an old dry-fly man during the fall, winter and even the cold, gray days of April when, so often, the streams are high, fast and roiled—dead for the dry-fly angler.

But, finally, the winds begin to soften; the days grow warmer; the buds start to open; the warblers and water thrushes arrive. Again, the dry-fly angler's world is alive, vibrant and full of color. When nature is at her prettiest, brown trout fishing is at its best.

95
Food

Finally, in late April, comes the long-awaited day. Looking up to the pool ahead, a winged form suddenly appears on the surface, apparently from nowhere. Fluttering for a brief moment, the fragile creature takes off upstream, in a slant like a plane. Another winged form appears, struggling to reach the surface from a gravel bed below. Then another, wings virtually sprouting, like the legerdemain of a magician, just as the fly pops from the water. Wing muscles preconditioned as they form; no previous flight training is necessary. Another winged creature emerges. And another. The first mayfly hatch of the season is on!

The family Ephemeridae—Greek for "lasting but a day"—has intrigued naturalists, poets, philosophers and fishermen for ages. As nymphs, mayflies may undergo as many as twenty molts during their underwater life. In their winged form, mayflies exhibit a remarkable peculiarity unlike any other insect. After seemingly assuming adult form, they molt once more, shedding a dull skin for a brighter, glistening coat.

Those mayflies I observed in the pool ahead were in the subimago stage—"duns" to us fly fishermen, the first winged form. Undergoing one more molt, they assume a final, or imago, stage of development—"spinners" in the lexicon of dry-fly angling.

Spinners are ready to mate. Males collect in hovering swarms over a pool or riff. Now and then, a female spinner flies into the swarm, getting caught up in their jet stream. Suddenly a male rushes at her, clasping her with his front legs, to fly away like an eloping couple to consummate the marriage. Copulation is immediate. Yawing a bit on their nuptial flight, the couple begin to lose altitude; the male unclasps and flies off ungallantly to court another mate.

Eggs fertilized, some female spinners, such as *Eph-*

emerella subvaria—Lady Beaverkill—jettison the entire egg mass in flight; others, such as *Ephemera guttulata*—Coffin Fly—dap the eggs off by touching the abdomen to the surface of the water. Sometimes a female mayfly goes below the surface of the water to deposit eggs on a stone.

From the time a mayfly becomes a flying insect its mouth begins to atrophy; during the entire winged stage the mayfly does not feed.

But a brown trout does—with gusto. Some nymphs are gobbled up on their way to the surface. Duns are snatched in that fluttering moment of hesitation before becoming airborne. Spinners during the dapping performance are often snapped up in a rhythmic syndrome. Eggs deposited, the spinner, spent and with wings outstretched, now floats helplessly downstream, an easy mark for the most lackadaisical brown trout. The final chance to gorge on that particular hatch.

A few seasons ago, Elsie Darbee, Catskill flytier, gave me a few Spent-Wing Royal Coachmans to try. The very first fishing trip made me realize what a fine fish-taker I'd been overlooking in nearly three decades of dry-fly fishing. Wonderfully effective at the end of a hatch, the pattern in size 18, I've found, is also a good "locater" fly during the summer doldrums.

At Cornell, I trained in entomology on "Needham and Needham,"[29] whose manual was the bible for would-be fisheries biologists. The Needhams' primer concentrated on the larval form of aquatic life, so I became acquainted with trout-stream animals, including mayflies, as crawling rather than winged creatures. Fortunately my professors were not the scholarly nitpickers lampooned in college humor. In the case of mayflies, with over five hundred species in the United States alone, teachers did not require students to key out specimens to species; it was academically acceptable if we could identify simply to genus.

Thus, I became familiar with an *Iron,* a *Stenonema* or an *Ephemerella* as mayfly nymphs before I knew them in their dry-fly, winged forms as Quill Gordon, Light Cahill or Hendrickson.

It was not the rarefied atmosphere of scholars but angling writers who helped to complete my education in fly-fishing entomology: Alfred Ronalds,[30] Preston J. Jennings,[31] Charles M. Wetzel,[32] and Arthur Flick[33] heading the list.

But, in the final analysis, it is the brown trout itself which keeps putting finishing touches on my schooling—schooling which continues to amaze me by its humbling gaps and the scores of lessons still to be learned.

One lesson I learned early in the game was the dominance of mayflies in the diet of a brown trout. Dr. Paul Needham,[34] in a scientific study a few decades ago, confirmed what fly fishermen have known since the days of Juliana Berners. In 1653, Izaak Walton noted: "The trout . . . especially he loves the may-flie; and these make the trout bold and lusty and he is usually fatter and better meat at the end of the month than at any other time of the year."

A glance at the chart shows that mayflies make up about 80 percent of the brown trout's food. Caddis flies come in a poor second, about 10 percent, while the remaining 10 percent represents a potpourri of a dozen or so food items—both aquatic and terrestrial.

Dr. Needham's work is especially significant because it applies to brown trout in sizes of interest to the angler. Specimens studied ranged from five inchès to twelve inches, the average length being about eight inches. Brown trout fry and fingerlings, of course, first

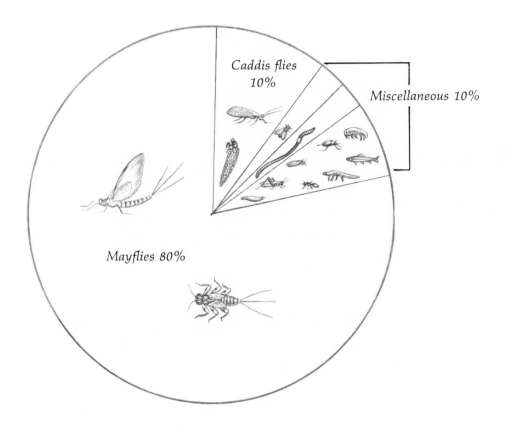

Caddis flies
10%

Miscellaneous 10%

Mayflies 80%

feed on plankton and the most minute of trout-stream fauna. But mayflies become an important food item at a surprisingly early age.

Of 2,404 items in the stomachs of brown trout, Dr. Needham identified 1,907 as mayflies. However, of the 1,907 mayflies, 1,714 were nymphs. Only 193 were duns or spinners.

Studies flyspecked with similar statistics by other fisheries scientists confirm Dr. Needham's findings. In the face of such incontrovertible evidence, dismaying to dry-fly fishermen, it is amazing that every brown trout angler does not use the nymph exclusively.

But somehow, the consecrated, card-carrying members of the guild prefer to stick to the dry fly despite the incredibly long odds on fishing's tote board.

Although the brown trout is a flamboyant opportunist—taking what food it can get when it can get it—Dr. Needham's forage ratios show that mayflies—nymphs, duns, spinners—are the staple diet items.

"Floating food is caviar; underwater food is beef to the brown trout," is the way Frederic Halford, English angler, flytier and fishing writer, put it almost a century ago.

What is caviar to the brown trout is cream-of-the-cream fishing to the angler who has a working knowledge of trout-stream entomology. Such knowledge puts a sharper edge on the sport, and *Salmo trutta*'s preference for Ephemeridae also adds an extra measure of poetry.

The brown trout and the mayfly—teamed up—make more than a delightful kind of fishing. They have created a unique social institution.

Management

The brown trout has been observed, studied and managed more than any other trout—more than any other game fish.

For years, management was more concerned with having brown trout to catch rather than catching brown trout. In its own hard-boiled jargon, management strives to establish an exploitable resource for the benefit of fishermen. Management deals with the findings of research: species suitability, carrying capacity, production, survival and harvesting yields. Management manipulates the factors—physical, chemical and biological—which govern brown trout populations.

More recently, management has focused sharply on "quality fishing"—not exactly a new term, but showing up more and more frequently in the thinking of fisheries biologists and fishermen.

Over the years, quality fishing has suggested different things to different people, a concept sometimes as difficult to pin down as mercury is to pick up.

For instance, when I came on the management scene in the 1930s as a fish hatchery worker, quality fishing was equated with quantity fishing: the more fish a fisherman caught, the better the fishing. It followed quite logically that the more fish stocked, the more fish caught. So compelling was this thesis that trout hatcheries ruled the management roost, here and abroad, for fifty years.

My salad days in fisheries work coincided with the era of the hatchery fixation. At the state hatchery at Rome, New York, where I worked, production was king. Specializing in brown trout, we were always striving to beat the previous year's output—a sizable figure of around seven million browns coming off the assembly line annually. For a guy who detests figures and flunked math more than once, the hatchery's production figures had a horrible fascination; I was continually checking the daily and monthly reports. The old-timers often kidded me about my "paper fish."

Near the end of my hatchery tour of duty, improved scientific methods began to replace some of the old-timers' homespun husbandry—mostly very good, too, not to be down-graded. However, significant management contributions—hatchery-oriented—were beginning to come out of many countries, chiefly Germany, England, Scotland and America. In the United States, trained scientists like New York's Tunison, Deuel and Haskell put trout nutrition on a highly scientific basis with diet formulae, which revolutionized the centuries-old practices of Dom Pinchon and the more recent methods of Seth Green and Fred Mather.

Quality fishing now took on a new meaning. Quality fishing meant a better product—a better hatchery trout. With the introduction of improved diets better balanced in proteins and carbohydrates and beefed up with vitamins, we hatchery workers dreamed of a new breed of hatchery-raised brown trout—a brown trout with even more gusto than a wild brown.

It proved to be like Don Quixote's impossible dream. In spite of increased production, in spite of a better product, quality fishing did not dominate the angling scene.

It was becoming increasingly clear that the fish hatchery was not the sole answer to better brown trout management. More and more fishermen began to wonder about the things that new breed of fisheries worker—the fisheries biologist—had been wondering about: What was happening to all those fish being planted year after year? Sometimes it seemed as if stocking not only failed to improve fishing but actually made it worse.

It was puzzling, too, that in some streams that were regularly stocked with brook trout, brown trout were showing up more and more in the catches. More disturbing were stream situations where trout had always thrived but bass were taking over.

Why? What were the answers? Fishermen asked the fish culturists. They did not know. Nor did the top-

103
Management

brass administrators. No one had the answers. It began to dawn on everyone that the situation needed a thorough study.

New York, a pioneer in the field of fish culture, was also the first state to swing into action on a comprehensive study of fishes in their natural habitats. In 1926, the state legislature appropriated $15,000—a tidy sum in those days—for a full-fledged biological survey.

There were no fisheries biologists in government in 1926, but a qualified group of scientists was recruited from universities in the United States and Canada. Headed up by Dr. Emmeline Moore, the New York Biological Survey was completed with unusual distinction and was recognized throughout the world as a landmark accomplishment in fisheries research and management.

The job required fourteen years to complete, under three different governors—Al Smith, Franklin Roosevelt and Herbert Lehman. Truly a miracle. In those times as today, fisheries studies did not have much sex appeal in the political arena, nor fisheries administrators much clout. Dr. Moore's stout defense kept the Biological Survey going—a program which served as a blueprint for sister state agencies and the federal government.

The Survey covered the whole spectrum of investigation but was often pointed in the direction of the brown trout because of its increasing importance in the trout-management picture. Data collected on a brown trout stream included stream length, width, depth, volume, velocity, pollution, competition of associated species, altitude, gradient, pool-riff ratio, water temperature, pH, oxygen content and a host of other factors which affect fish populations. An enormous amount of basic information can be gathered in an amazingly short time. The going gets tougher in the analyzing and evaluating stages.

The findings of these studies helped do away with many of the blundering trial-and-error methods of trout-stream management. In New York, the Biological Survey's greatest contribution was a realistic stocking policy for every trout stream in the state.

Brown trout management was put on a sounder basis by gearing stocking to the stream's carrying capacity and angling pressure, planting hatchery stock of the most appropriate sizes and numbers, enabling hatcheries to adjust production to actual requirements, preventing the stocking of unsuitable or harmful species, recommending fishing regulations tailored to conditions and pointing up situations where there was a need for further study.

Looking back at fisheries management today, the value of the trout-management practices across the nation has been demonstrated again and again. It is not being overly dramatic to say that trout management was on the edge of biological brinkmanship at the height of trial-and-error methods of fifty years ago.

Moreover, the money saved in more efficient stocking has paid for the cost of the Biological Survey many times. Before the Survey's findings were put into effect, most trout streams were stocked beyond their capacities to support the trout planted. Countless thousands of hatchery trout were wasted—like continuing to pour water into a pail after it is full.

But too much was expected of these studies. In New York and other states, biological surveys had to be oversold to get annual operating funds. In desperation, claims beyond a survey's capabilities were made.

Fishermen began to think of surveys as an ivory-tower boondoggle. But a load of big hatchery browns dumped in their favorite stream—now that was real trout management in action.

Even before the New York Biological Survey was completed it was dubbed the Diabolical Survey. Fishermen were especially disgruntled by the elimination of the ancient "application system" in which all a fisherman needed to do to get hatchery trout was to fill out a form. In line with Survey recommendations, trout were now assigned to the stream itself, the number and size tailored to the stream's carrying capacity.

The Survey helped to shift the focus of attention in fisheries management from the hatchery to the habitat. Although the hatchery fixation was hard to shake—"Just keep raising more fish and dump 'em in"—even a casually observant fisherman could not help but notice that the "dumping-in" places had changed and not for the better.

Even in the 1920s, signs of environmental deterioration were beginning to show up. Poor land-use practices, as overgrazing by stock, caused severe erosion of trout-stream banks, resulting in silting—the ruin of spawning beds and a reduced food supply.

Overcutting of timber, besides contributing to erosion, exposed long stretches of water to the direct rays of the sun, frequently sending water temperatures beyond the toleration limit of even the hardy brown trout.

Fisheries biologists who had been working closely with the environment on surveys began to think in terms of the environment, adding a new ingredient to trout management. If the environment could be restored, they reasoned—or better yet, improved—nature and the trout would respond in kind. Another approach to create quality fishing was born: trout-stream improvement.

Actually trout-stream improvement started in England. But in this country, Michigan led the way, beginning in the 1930s under the leadership of Dr. Albert S.

Hazzard, a New York Biological Survey alumnus. Dr. Hazzard, however, with true professional courtesy, insists that Edward R. Hewitt,[35] Dr. Carl L. Hubbs,[36] Dr. Clarence M. Tarzwell and others were more responsible for its growth in America.

Looking back on its beginnings, Al Hazzard told me recently: "I have always felt that environmental improvement is the best way to increase the natural production of trout. Of course it should start with the watershed to check erosion of the soil and to protect and restore the banks. Maintaining suitable bank cover is also vital in temperature control and contributes to food production. Siltation is the greatest destroyer of spawning beds as well as food-producing areas. Pools and hides are essential to good brown trout production. The number of 'homes' for browns of various sizes determines the trout population as well as the fishing spots. Stream improvement benefits both fish and fishermen."

New York was another pioneer in trout-stream improvement, first under Emerson James and then under Maurice B. Otis, who directed a remarkable degree of sophisticated thinking to the development of man-made devices.

Fishermen took to the stream-improvement idea with an enthusiasm seldom bestowed on fisheries biologists' activities. This was not a white-coat, laboratory experiment; not esoteric research but something tangible, something practical.

Again, here was management in action, here was quality fishing in the making: a V dam to concentrate the flow of the stream, a boon to dry-fly fishing; a stone-filled log riprap to stabilize a stream bank; a straight-log dam providing a new living room; a single-wing deflector to control the course of a stream; a double-wing deflector to speed up stream flow or scour the bottom to

STREAM IMPROVEMENT STRUCTURES

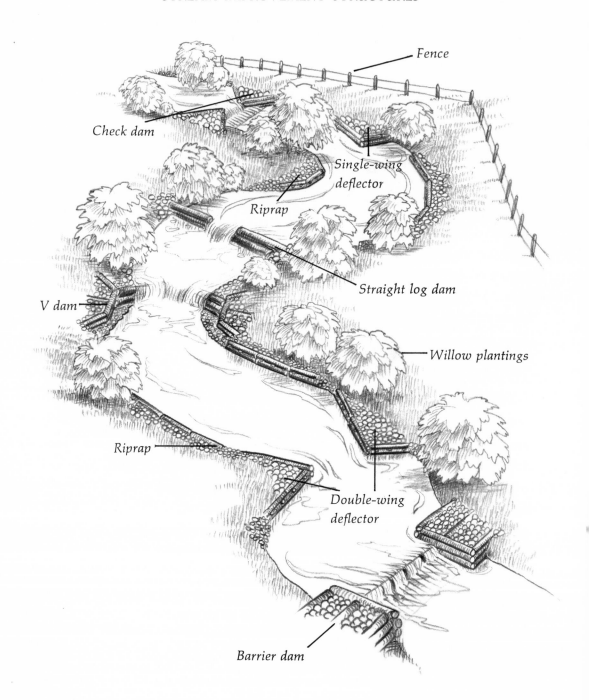

Fence

Check dam

Single-wing deflector

Riprap

Straight log dam

V dam

Willow plantings

Riprap

Double-wing deflector

Barrier dam

expose a spawning site; a check dam in the headwaters to reduce silting downstream; a barrier dam downstream to help prevent undesirable species of fish from moving upstream; willow plantings to provide shade and a root mass to check bank erosion; and fenced streambank strips to keep out livestock and reduce the crumbling of the edges of pasture trout streams.

All structures to which brown trout respond by growing bigger, and more plentiful.

But in time—as happened with trout hatcheries, and as happened with biological surveys—disappointment with stream-improvement programs began to show up. Not that stream-improvement structures, soundly designed and properly placed, did not fulfill their functions. Mostly they did their job well. In Michigan, where careful "before-and-after" records were kept for three years before the installation of structures and three years after, the total yield of trout soared 138 percent!

But improved fishing is often a self-defeating proposition. Anglers are endowed with an uncanny, built-in radar that beams back a new fishing hot spot the moment it is born. The increase in fishing pressure—on one Michigan stream, pressure jumped 81 percent—often nullifies benefits to the individual angler.

Fisheries management budgets, too, soon revealed that stream improvement is not a cheap way to better fishing. Again in Michigan, a cost-benefit analysis showed that in terms of trout added to the creel, the program cost was $1.43 per fish.

But the main reason for a leveling-off in fishermen's enthusiasm for stream improvement was the plain fact that the program fell short of that elusive goal of both fishermen and fisheries biologists—quality fishing.

Yet quality fishing, however elusive, as a goal of fisheries management, has not lost its challenge. Fishermen and fisheries biologists, undaunted by disappointment after disappointment, keep searching for the hidden key.

In the United States, where public rather than private fishing dominates angling, the path has led back to the very first tools of fisheries management—laws and regulations.

The path also turns back to the ubiquitous brown trout, which sparks the revival of regulations. Regulations, however, not designed, as in the past, just to restrict the fisherman's activities but to enhance his angling experience.

The first fishing regulations date back about eight hundred years, when Scotland enacted laws restricting the use of nets, or "engines" as they were called. In America, the first protective legal measure was a closed season to protect a species through at least one spawning. Later the closed season was backed up by a minimum size limit to permit a trout to attain a length at which it is sexually mature.

This concept, applied to the brown trout and most other species, is one of those half-truths which obscure the real issue: Is the closed-season/size-limit formula effective in permitting the species to maintain sufficient numbers of trout in sizes to provide satisfactory fishing?

With typical 20–20 hindsight and today's improved knowledge of fisheries biology, it is not difficult to spot some of the fallacies in these long-established, widely used basic regulations: closed seasons and size limits. For instance, the harvesting of small immature brown trout is not harmful if there is an excess of such individuals in a population unit. In fact, I know many small mountain streams where brown trout are so abundant they crowd the pools. Here the conventional 6- or 7-inch size limit is actually harmful. Far better management would be to cut the resident stock drastically to reduce competition for space and food. A saucer of milk adequate for four kittens is going to make slim pickings if eight kittens gather around the dish. Incidentally, these small brown trout are not genetically "stunted" as formerly believed. Experiments in which small brown trout were captured and placed in hatcheries show they grow normally on hatchery diets.

In put-and-take brown trout fishing, efficient management encourages intensive harvesting of large, costly trout. Here a size limit defeats the purpose of stocking for the rod. Nor can statewide size limits take into full consideration the variation in the growth rates of brown trout in different waters. Fishermen are aware of the enormous difference in the growth of lake browns and stream browns, and in less spectacular fashion, the growth rate of stream browns often varies from stream to stream.

Another much overlooked factor in the brown trout size-limit picture is the difference in size and age at which male and female brown trout are first capable of reproduction.

Except for the precocious individuals, male brown trout become sexually mature near the end of their second year when length ranges from 5 to 7 inches. But female browns do not reach sexual maturity until their third year at a length of 8 to 10 inches. Thus, while the commonly used size limits of 6 to 8 inches protect most male brown trout, they do not afford much protection to the females.

Fisheries biologists, further analyzing the effects of size limits, began to question their value as an overall management measure. New York and Maine, for instance, balancing the ecological and sociological equities, shelved statewide size limits on trout over a decade ago. Nothing has happened to justify a return to a minimum size limit. The elimination of the size limit may not have improved trout fishing noticeably, but it certainly has demonstrated that it was a needless restriction.

But the perennial quest for quality fishing has uncovered some hidden values of regulations as a tool of trout management. The new use of regulations leans less on biology and more on sociology. Today's trout-fishing regulations are more a code of conduct than measures to protect the species within the framework of rigid biological concepts.

I recall a fellow worker coming into the office after a night of being clobbered at a fishermen's club meeting. There's no closed season on fisheries biologists. Slumping down at his desk, he muttered: "What we need is fishermen management, not fisheries management."

The day of fishermen management is here. Strangely enough, the main thrust of the new approach comes from fishermen themselves. A growing number of anglers are willing to *restrict* their sport to *improve* their sport. In this country, over-generous creel limits have favored the meat fishermen. One of the first efforts in America to curtail the fish hog was put into effect on two top-drawer Catskill streams when they were part of my beat as a fisheries biologist in the 1940s and 1950s. Nudged by a coterie of dedicated Catskill anglers, I was able to help in getting the daily creel limit on the Beaver Kill and Willowemoc reduced from ten to five trout.

Cutting the fish hog down to size was a big step forward not only in sportsmanship but also in fisheries management, helping to spread the available resource among more fishermen.

It was not long before a strong movement developed in many of the trout states to go a step further: setting aside areas where *all* trout caught had to be released and returned to the water. It was a revolutionary idea at the time. Again the Beaver Kill and Willowemoc were in the vanguard, as was Pennsylvania with Fisherman's Paradise on Spring Creek. To make the task of unhooking and releasing easier, Maryland (Savage River and Deer Creek) and West Virginia (Back Fork of Elk River and Shavers Fork) put in a regulation requiring the use of barbless hooks on their "catch and release" areas—streams soon to be known all over the country as "fishing-for-fun" waters.

When fishing-for-fun projects were first being considered, there was considerable support from anglers and administrators to restrict fishing to fly fishing only. However, opinion in many states was divided, non-fly fishermen putting up stiff resistance. In some states a compromise was worked out in which fishing in selected areas was restricted to the use of artificial lures only.

Long ago, Austria and South Africa banned the use of live bait in trout waters. Today, Maine lists over 250 waters where it is illegal to use live bait. The prohibition of live bait in trout waters, a biological measure, serves management by helping to keep harmful species of fish from being introduced. On the sociological side of the management ledger, Pennsylvania, Maryland and North Carolina have been successful in banning spinning on several brown trout streams.

A large bloc of fishermen grumbled about the emphasis on trout in the new fisheries management, complaining that they were getting the short end of the fish pole and that in most trout states their license money was going for trout management.

However, enough trout fishermen were willing to pay more for their sport and did not object to the extra bite of a special-use license, known generally through-out the country as a "trout stamp." A growing number of states have adopted this modified revenue-sharing plan. At the last count, of the thirty-eight states which enjoy brown trout fishing, Arizona, California, Delaware, Georgia, Indiana, Iowa, Missouri, Nebraska, New Jersey, Tennessee, Virginia and West Virginia had adopted the trout stamp as a trout-management measure. Nebraska has an ingenious management gimmick—a daily trout-fishing tag. Arizona has reciprocal arrangements with its neighbors, California and Nevada, which require a special-use stamp for fishing in certain boundary waters.

As trout fishing solely for sport replaces meat fishing, more and more anglers are accepting the idea of *catching* trout but not *keeping* trout. In the changeover, too, anglers are discovering the delights of fly fishing. Anglers all over the country give hearty support to the "fly-fishing-only" areas in their states.

A pioneer in promoting the fly-fishing-only idea was Pennsylvania, which has set aside fly-fishing-only sections on thirty-eight of its best trout streams—sections which total up to over a hundred miles, mostly brown trout water.

Maine lists over 150 fly-fishing-only waters mostly ponds, but also sections on some fine streams like the Kennebago and Rangeley rivers. Other states which have set aside such areas include Connecticut, Colorado, Delaware, Maryland, Massachusetts, Michigan, Tennessee, Washington and Wisconsin—again, mostly brown trout streams.

Quality fishing as an idea and ideal continues to dominate the dialogue of both fishermen and fisheries administrators. The concept is now firmly embedded in the fisheries-management structure. The states of New

York in the East and Washington in the West now actually list "Quality Fishing" in their regulations syllabus given to fishermen when they purchase a fishing license.

In the new quality-oriented trout management, general size limits, abandoned by a score or more of states, are being revived in individual situations as a management tool to promote the new idea of trophy trout fishing. Now the goal is a stream where trophy trout add to the excitement of angling.

For example, in New York, on the West Branch of the Ausable River, my trout stream during the Depression of the 1930s, a 14-inch size limit is in force; on Maryland's Savage River, restricted to the use of artificial flies with a single barbless hook, one trout over 15 inches may be kept per day; on sections of New Mexico's San Juan River—artificial lures only—the minimum size limit is also 15 inches; North Carolina has designated Lost Cove Creek, sections of the Nantahala River, South Mills River and Wilson Creek as Trophy Trout Waters on which the minimum size limit on brown trout is 16 inches; on West Virginia's Catch-and-Release Streams—Back Fork of Elk River and Shavers Fork—the size limit for trout is 18 inches; Colorado, which has outdistanced all the other states in a biosocio classification of its trout waters (Artificial Fly and Lure Waters Only, Catch-and-Release Waters and Special Trophy Waters), two sections of the Arkansas River have been placed in the latter category—sections where all trout between 10 inches and 20 inches must be returned to the water; on Pennsylvania's Yellow Breeches Creek and several other Fish-for-Fun streams, the minimum size limit is 20 inches; and Georgia tops all the states in refurbishing size limits—a section of Waters Creek, open only on weekends, carries a minimum size limit on trout of 22 inches!

Such highly specialized fisheries management, of course, sometimes applies to other species of trout, but it is *Salmo trutta* with its inherent proclivity for prodigious growth which gets top billing in most of the trophy trout waters in this country.

One might suppose that fisheries management had at last achieved its goal. But looking back at various steps on the trout-management ladder—trout hatcheries, biological surveys, habitat improvement and laws and regulations—I recall that each stage, in turn, was thought to be the answer to quality trout fishing.

I suspect the sociological approach has advanced to about the level of biology in the days of Seth Green. Sociology with an amazing web of interrelationships has an ecology all its own.

Indeed, in the recent emphasis on the sociological approach, ecology has been given a secondary role in the fisheries-management complex. The continuous change of conditions in the brown trout's aquatic habitat points out the need for a continuing professional evaluation of the environment, too.

Whatever the fisheries-management gimmicks to come, I will continue to bet on the brown trout. With its enduring viability and will to survive, I am confident *Salmo trutta* will be around to manage for a long time to come.

Ecology

An environment which is good for *Salmo trutta* is good for *Homo sapiens.* Over three hundred years ago, Izaak Walton recognized his favorite fish's environmental requirements:" . . . the trout is a Fish that feeds clean and purely in the swiftest streams and hardest gravel . . . and the most dainty pallates have allowed precedency to him."

Indeed, the brown trout is one of nature's best environmental barometers. A brown in a stream, like a canary in a coal mine, serves as a telltale indicator organism, its behavior often warning of brewing biological troubles ahead.

When I started my professional career in conservation nearly forty years ago, the signs were going up that the American environment was on its way to hell in an ecological handbasket. Few of us, if any, noticed. None of us gave the broad picture any thought because we did not realize there was a broad picture. True, we were familiar with today's household word "ecology." Dr. Paul Needham was teaching a course called "Ecology" at Cornell back in 1928. But in those days, even ecology was viewed in narrower terms. We confined our viewpoint to our particular academic discipline under the broad umbrella of "biology."

Conditioned by my academic training, I have a tendency to hold to the more literal translation of "ecology": from the Greek, *oikos* meaning "home" and *logia* "the study of." More practically, the relation of an organism to its environment.

The brown trout's ideal home is a well-balanced ecological niche which provides the essentials of life: food, shelter and facilities for reproduction. But today as the catalogue of environmental horrors grows, *Salmo trutta* is caught in the inexorable squeeze between an expanding population and a contracting environment.

The brown's habitat reacts to every environmental change:

Drain a headwater marsh and the cold, life-supporting feeder streams are destroyed. A priceless trout stream dies aborning.

Channelize a watercourse and the basic requirements of a trout's existence are obliterated.

Put a housing development on a hillside and the nearby trout stream becomes a storm sewer.

Clear-cut woodlands on a watershed and a chain reaction results—erosion, flooding, silting.

It doesn't require a computerized analysis to understand that the brown trout community is made up and controlled by a complex set of interrelated physical, chemical and biological factors.

Of all the ingredients which make up the brown trout complex, water, obviously, is the most important. Just as the spring water of a "wee burn" is a basic component of choice Scotch whisky, so that same pure water helps produce fine Loch Leven trout.

My first fishing mentor, whose Indian blood endowed him with an instinctive sense for evaluating nature, once said while kneeling on the edge of a crystal-clear pool on the Rondout, "I wouldn't eat a trout from a brook I wouldn't take a drink from."

His words were prophetic. Today, not far from that pristine spot, Merriman Dam bottles up Rondout Reservoir, a unit in New York City's vast water-supply system, providing water to eight million thirsty Gothamites.

My mountain-man friend had an affinity for fishing and firewater—"Old Overalls" we kids called his favorite brand. A patient of my doctor father—mostly for dreams of pink snakes—he worked off his bills doing yard work. At garden-planting time we would spade enough ground to get a supply of worms and then head for the Rondout. Both of us played hooky so often that my father felt the senior partner was a bad influence on me and liquidated the syndicate. After that I became pretty much of a loner on trout streams. A custom which has continued.

Although *Salmo trutta* shows a tolerance for relatively high water temperatures, it is still classified as a cold-water animal. At the Cornell Fish Hatchery Laboratory, Dr. George Embody ran tests on the temperature toleration limits of local species of trout. Brook trout folded at 75° F.; browns at 81°; and rainbows at 83°. Typically, there was some evidence that browns could hold out a little longer at the toleration limit than either brooks or rainbows.

In my own field-testing, I have found I've had the best brown trout fishing when water temperatures ranged from 64° to 68° F.—temperatures which usually prevail in May and June in most of the trout streams in the northeastern United States. In this region brown trout fishing usually goes into the doldrums during July and August, but during cool summers, 64° to 68° F. are again the magic numbers, as they are in September in New York, where early fall fishing is permitted.

It is significant, I think, that many states use some of the requirements of trout in establishing the classification of water-quality standards. For example, the health departments of most states require a minimum of five parts per million of dissolved oxygen for both trout waters and drinking water.

How intricately woven is the ecological web of the brown trout! Certain species of mayflies—*Salmo trutta*'s principal food—are equally susceptible to low-oxygen stress. It is interesting to note that the ever popular Hendrickson *(Ephemerella subvaria)* is the least tolerant of all the species of mayflies—another excellent indicator organism in evaluating a brown trout stream.

In my field days as a fisheries biologist we were on the lookout for another indicator organism on streams where pollution was suspected. The critter is the rat-tailed maggot, larva of the drone fly, a two-winged fly which looks not unlike a male honey bee. The rat-tailed maggot is able to survive in water depleted of oxygen by means of its telescopic air tube, which projects above the surface of the water to get good air.

The acid/alkaline content of water is important to the well-being of the brown trout. What happens in the blood of *Salmo trutta* in adjusting to different waters, either acid or alkaline, is not fully understood. On the conventional pH scale—7.0 being neutral with readings below 7.0 an index of acidity and above 7.0 of alkalinity—the blood of a brown trout registers around 7.1.

When water has a pH value less than the pH of trout blood it contains an excess of free hydrogen ions which diffuse rapidly through gill membranes. This causes the consumption of extra energy, probably affecting the trout's metabolism, which slows up growth. In streams where the pH value of water is above the pH of trout blood, there is an excess of OH ions, which diffuse through the gills much more slowly and therefore are more easily regulated within the trout's internal economy.

Experience has taught fisheries biologists that brown trout are at odds with their environments when pH readings drop below 5.0 or exceed 9.0.

Many trout streams reveal a wide range of pH values in different sections. The Beaver Kill, for instance, has a pH of 6.6 as it spills down Doubletop Mountain; at the Junction Pool in Roscoe, 7.2; and at its mouth in East Branch, 8.8.

The ideal pH range for good growth and good fishing appears to be between 6.8 and 7.8. In my salad days as a fisheries biologist I learned the importance of pH in hatchery stocking operations.

Brown trout raised in alkaline waters have some difficulty in making the required physiological adjustment when planted in acid waters. Indeed, some trout, especially young fingerlings, never make it.

Nature, on her own, can throw an ecological curve—sometimes physical, sometimes biological.

Hurricanes are awesome physical forces of destruction. Less dramatic than the loss of human life is the devastation of other living organisms. For example, a late-fall hurricane in 1951 took a heavy toll of Catskill trout streams—especially the Rondout, Neversink and Esopus—taking out dozens of bridges and dams, and destroying long sections of trout habitat.

Another cause of spectacular destruction is a heavy accumulation of anchor ice in a trout stream.

I remember a day on the Beaver Kill when, after a record-breaking cold winter, a sudden spring thaw caused the ice to let go within a few hours, sending thousands of tons of ice cakes cascading down to the Delaware River. Surprisingly enough, the following fishing season showed the hardy brown trout had withstood the crushing avalanche amazingly well. Some scientists believe that trout blocked off from their usual homes hug the bottom where the velocity of currents is much reduced. A physical phenomenon similar to surface tension; like that layer of dust which remains on the hood of a car even though it is speeding at seventy miles per hour.

However, there were indications that insect life did not survive so well: few hatches in fewer numbers. Perhaps this scarcity was the reason the fishing was so good that season. Those Beaver Kill browns were real hungry!

Nature also goes on frequent biological rampages, although it is often difficult to sort out the natural from the man-made causes and effects. Even eutrophication, the natural aging of a body of water, a symptom of which is the increased growth of algae and aquatic plants, is probably accelerated by nutrients in man-made detergents especially rich in phosphates.

Fishermen have learned about "algae blooms" in ponds and slow-moving sections of trout streams which take place during the summer months—growths so prodigious at times that the dissolved oxygen content of the water is reduced to the lethal point.

Algae is a bane of angling life, fouling up flies and making footing treacherous. In my Lake Placid days, wading the West Branch of the Ausable at certain times during the summer was like walking on greased cannon balls.

"Winter kill" is also a fairly common phenomenon of nature. Thick ice and a heavy snow cover shut out sunlight, arresting the usual photosynthetic process so that aquatic vegetation, ordinarily giving off oxygen during the daylight hours and carbon dioxide at night, gives off carbon dioxide continually, resulting in mortalities, most of which go unobserved.

Nature's caprices create havoc, but so does man in his desire to dominate the environment. A brown trout habitat is a highly sensitive mechanism. Fallout from nuclear testing in Siberia, in its eastward drift, may show up in the trout streams of Canada's prairie provinces.

It may not be too farfetched to forecast that the indiscriminate use of a long-lasting, hard-core pesticide like DDT applied to Montana lands draining into the Missouri River would follow down the Mississippi to the Gulf of Mexico and thence in the Gulf Stream to the waters off the British Isles to produce sterility in sea-run brown trout.

Every avenue of approach to a better knowledge of *Salmo trutta* brings into sharper focus the infinite variety of its interrelationships—relationships that add a compelling fascination to the whole brown trout complex.

Eugene V. Connett,[37] angler, writer, publisher—all *par excellence*—put it so well: "I am satisfied that nothing can take the place of a real knowledge of the trout we fish for—how they live, how they see, what makes them do what they do when they do it."

The brown trout does not live by itself nor for itself. Besides insects, crustaceans and amphibians, *Salmo trutta* shares its ecological niche with other finny associates.

In field checks of trout streams a fisheries biologist may have difficulty in capturing trout specimens, so he is on the lookout for the fresh-water sculpin, also known as the miller's thumb and more frequently as the muddler. This little fellow, lacking an air bladder, hugs the bottom of the stream and is seldom seen by fishermen. Just as the brown trout is a good indicator of the aquatic environment, so the muddler is evidence that a stream is potential trout water. The muddler is an important diet item of trout in the larger, economy sizes. And the artificial muddler minnow fly is one of the most deadly of trout lures. In action, the muddler may also resemble a Johnny darter, a species in another family of fishes, important to brown trout at a fish-eating age and size.

Various members of the minnow family (Cyprinidae) are frequently joint tenants in the brown trout community, the most ubiquitous and abundant being the black-nosed dace, another important food item of big browns.

Long food chains, incidentally, make a fisheries biologist aware of ecology early in the game: microscopic plant and animal plankton provide food for tiny insects and crustaceans, which, in turn, become part of the diet of larger insects, crustaceans and small fish, and so on in

124
The Compleat Brown Trout

a graduated scale up to the lunker browns which can make a meal of a good-sized keeper-trout.

A feathered imitation of the black-nosed dace tied as a bucktail to resemble the male in breeding colors—a bright splash of red on its sides—is almost as successful as the muddler in luring wily old browns.

The fallfish—chub or chavender, as Izaak Walton called it—is another neighbor of the brown trout. Walton said, "The chub is the worst Fish that swimmes." Completely lacking in fear or wile, the chub, the bane of fly fishing, invariably beats the more cautious brown to a floating fly. The first rush often fools a fisherman into thinking he has hooked a good trout. But after a moment of foolish, frenetic thrashing, the chub poops out.

The common sucker, abundant in many trout streams, gets along well with the brown and causes no problems for fishermen.

Both the sucker and the sculpin—the mouth of the black-nosed dace is too small—prey on the eggs of brown trout at spawning time. However, the female brown does a good job of intercepting raids and soon covers the eggs in the nest with gravel. Dr. John Greeley in his study of the spawning habits of trout in Michigan concluded that egg predation is not enough to be harmful.

In general, *Salmo trutta* coexists with the environmental chums nature has provided better than *Homo sapiens* does with his fellow citizens in the society he has created.

One case of incompatibility involves the aggressive small-mouthed bass. In lakes, both bass and brown trout get along quite well, each living in separate ecological compartments most of the year. But in streams where the two species share space and food, the contest is a stand-off: the brown trout population declines and the small-mouthed bass become stunted.

A showcase example of the disastrous effects of a

mixed population of trout and bass in a brown trout stream is the Catskill's Schoharie Creek, great love of Art Flick. When Gilboa Dam bottled up some five miles of the Schoharie to create another unit of the New York City water supply system, Devasego Falls, a natural barrier against bass infiltration, was submerged, defiling what was virtually a pure culture of trout above the falls. In attempts to control the intruders, special regulations permit the taking of small-mouthed bass in any size and any numbers from April 1 through November 30.

The life-supporting potential of a trout stream is best gauged by its carrying capacity, usually measured in the annual number of pounds of fish produced. Poundage may comprise a few species or many; poundage may be distributed among a number of small-sized fish or fewer bigger fish. Studies of the population dynamics of trout streams show that the poundage produced each year remains approximately the same if the conditions which govern the environment remain stable.

In the current global environmental crisis, the reform crusaders in their instant ecological programs have not focused much attention on the brown trout. But under the professional umbrella of a few old-fashioned fisheries biologists, helped by the amazing vitality of the fish itself, *Salmo trutta* is not listed as an endangered species.

Thriving best in the idyllic settings of Walton's England or Thoreau's America, this magnificent sporting fish is also found within sight of factory smokestacks and high-rise apartments.

I go along with Colin Fletcher, who, a few years ago, stated: "With the spread of modern civilization, industry moves outward from the cities and populations increase. For reasons perhaps not yet fully understood, brown trout withstand the new conditions better than other species. It seems to me that if present trends continue, browns are destined to be the trout of the future."

127
Ecology

✳

Tackle

The brown trout with its affinity for a floating fly brought a new and fascinating kind of angling to America—dry-fly fishing.

It all started in New York's Catskill Mountains, a region interlaced with fabulous trout streams: the Neversink, Beaver Kill, Willowemoc, Esopus, Schoharie, Rondout and Delaware.

Salmo trutta, the naturalized citizen, soon demonstrated that the wet-fly techniques used in taking the easy-to-catch brook trout simply did not work with the hard-to-catch brown. The dry-fly approach inspired new editions of rods, reels, lines and lures. The dry-fly angler's equipment gradually became an arsenal of efficiency.

Of the trinity of trappings—rod, reel, line—the rod is the basic tool. A brown trout, of course, can be caught on any kind of rod. Or a cane pole or a cut stick. But such implements should be reserved for sittin'-and-spittin' fishin'—a pleasant pastime and not to be scorned as an antidote for today's frenetic pace. But sittin'-and-spittin' fishin' is not the exciting sport that *Salmo trutta* has made possible.

A dry-fly angler seeking the brown trout in the fast-water streams of America needs a rod with stiffer action. A rod with a lot of backbone. The soft, willowy action of the buggy whips of the brook trout/wet-fly days simply could not cut it.

The first American fly rods were made in the days when bamboo reigned supreme. Samuel Phillipe, an Easton, Pennsylvania, gunsmith, was making bamboo rods of three, four and six strips as early as 1845. Dr. Alvin R. Grove, Jr.,[38] notes, however, that Phillipe used ash in some sections of a rod.

In the 1870s, Hiram Leonard of Bangor, Maine, perfected the all-bamboo, six-strip rod. In addition to his skill as an artisan, Leonard had a talent for attracting other gifted workmen to his shop—craftsmen such as Ed Payne, Fred Thomas and Billy Edwards, all of whom in time set up shops of their own.

Ed Payne established a plant in Highland Mills, New York, a gateway to the Catskills trout streams where the brown trout was gaining a reputation as a great game fish. Leonard had already located at nearby

Central Valley. Jim Payne, Ed's son, joined his father as a young man. Rods with the Payne imprint—requiring two months and forty-five operations to produce—spanned a period of sixty years.

Roy Steenrod, Catskill flytier, a close friend of Theodore Gordon's and a fellow worker when I was with the New York State Conservation Department, recounts a bit of fly-rod history which unfolded on one of the famous Catskill trout streams:

"In the spring of 1918 I was fishing on the Esopus with A. E. Hendrickson, George Stevenson and Jim Payne, the rod maker.

"During the lunch break we got talking rods and how they should have more pep for dry-fly work. A. E. spoke up and said he had a three-piece light salmon rod in the car that might be right. We all gave it a try but agreed it was too much rod. Taking it apart, I gave the middle joint and tip a few flicks.

" 'There, Jim,' I said, 'put a fly-rod grip on that and you'll have the dry-fly rod we've been looking for.'

"Jim gave it a try and replied, 'I can make a better rod than that.'

"And Jim did. He made a rod for each of us, using different-colored windings on each rod so we could tell them apart. I still have mine—9-foot, 6-ounce—a pretty heavy rod in today's thinking. When Theodore Gordon started fishing our Catskill streams, he was using a 10-foot, 10-ounce rod—a Hardy Perfection, I think." A short rod, I might add, compared to the 12- to 18-footers used by Juliana Berners and Charles Cotton.

Jim Payne compounded hundreds of rod patterns after that, varying rod action to fit different conditions—and the whimsical ideas of fishermen. But Roy believes that day on the Esopus in 1918 marked the beginning of a rod constructed especially for dry-fly fishing.

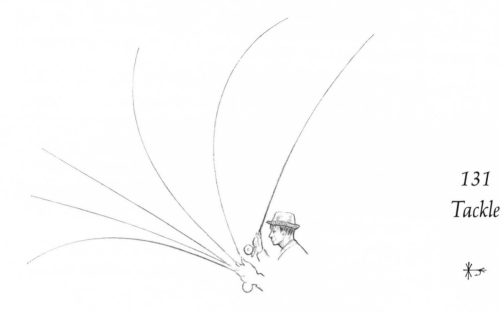

One time I was sitting in Jim Payne's shop during a March blizzard. The curing oven—used in tempering bamboo—was giving out a cheery warmth.

"That oven caused quite a problem a few years ago," recalled Jim. "Somehow my wife found the oven cooked the best pot of beans this side of Boston. The word got around among the neighbors and soon we seemed to be cooking beans more than making rods. I was a pretty unpopular guy around here when I put a stop to it."

In those days when well-heeled dry-fly anglers got a hankering for a fine fly rod, they would make pilgrimages to the shops of Payne, Leonard, Thomas, Edwards, Garrison, Powell, Orvis, Gillum, Phillipson, Uslan, Stoner, Young and other rod makers. There they could get a rod endowed with the distilled beauty of craftsmanship, made to their requirements in the manner of a Savile Row tailor who puts a customer in a saddle on a dummy horse to ensure the proper fit of a hacking jacket. As Oscar Wilde contended, "Give me the luxuries of life and I will get along without the necessities."

George La Branche went along with the Savile Row approach. "Selecting a rod," he said, "is as personal as buying a pair of gloves."

Wes Jordan, long the master rod builder at Orvis, translated this thought into action. With the angler's glove as a model, he could precisely position thumb and palm-heel indentations on the cork grip. A nicety still available at Orvis.

Wes, who once helped me on a magazine story, emphasized the full-curve principle in his rods—the rod bending evenly throughout its length from tip to butt under maximum load.

George La Branche, probably the best American logician ever to enter the angling circle, warned that "weight, balance, action, must suit the casting style of the user or he will not use it well or find it comfortable."

Charles Ritz[39] strongly advised anglers "to select a rod during the fishing season, not off season and after several days of fishing, because arm and wrist must be in proper training before sound judgment is possible."

Speaking for the distaff side of the dry-fly membership, Julia Fairchild, a founder and long-time president of The Woman Flyfisher's Club, recommends a fly rod of 7 to 8 feet and weighing from 2½ to 3¾ ounces.

Dame Julia, whom I've watched conquer a Neversink brown in masterful style, warns her sex: "The first and most important thing to do is reject firmly any and all offers of rods from well-meaning husbands, relatives and friends."

I've been wedded to bamboo since the beginning. My first rod—after a five-cent bamboo pole—was an Abbey & Imbrie 9-footer weighing probably close to 6 ounces. I caught my first brown trout on this rod. Actually the rod belonged to my father, who was invariably too busy to fish. Eventually, I acquired the rod by what I believe the legal profession calls "adverse possession."

Over the years I acquired several fine rods. But five years ago, I indulged myself with an Orvis Flea rod, a tiny wand 6½ feet long and weighing exactly 2 ounces. Matched with a two-ounce Hardy Flyweight reel and a Cortland 4-weight line, the little rod has added new dimensions and new pleasures in my quest for the brown trout.

I believe it was Henry Van Dyke who said: "The bamboo rod has lost in weight but gained in spirit."

The reel, or "wheele" which Izaak Walton mentioned in the second edition of his book, is still used chiefly by most anglers as a place to store line not in use, much the same as it was when the master fished for brown trout in seventeenth-century England. Even anglers skilled enough to use a stripping basket need a storage bin for the backing.

The Hawkeye reel that came with my first rod would do a satisfactory job on any brown trout stream today. Also put out by Abbey & Imbrie, the reel was a single-action skeleton-type and had a sliding click with just the right decibel count. And with enough tension to prevent line overrun when a brown stopped suddenly after the first run with the bait, a feature some modern reels lack.

My father was a country doctor—a horse-and-buggy man—in the days our family lived in the Catskills. I often went along with him, especially on trips up the Rondout. I fished with the boys of the family while father attended his patients. In exchange for being

taken to the best fishing holes, I let the boys use my "store tackle."

Accustomed to fishing with a cut stick, they would exclaim: "Gee, that's some pole and winder—works slick as a mink!"

One of the much overlooked functions of a reel is its role as a balancer—an especially important factor in dry-fly fishing for browns. One time on a working trip to the Catskills I had an unexpected opportunity to fish the evening rise. I had a rod in the car but no reel. Walt Dette, one of the original members of the Catskill School of Flytiers, and a good samaritan, loaned me his Hardy St. George, a much heavier reel than I ordinarily used with the rod—a 9-footer and a tiresome rod to cast. I was amazed at the ease and comfort of casting the same rod with Walt's heavier reel acting as a counterbalance and perfect pivot.

If all you want from fishing is fish, I suppose the line and hook are the most important pieces of equipment. Handlining for trout was an accepted method of sport fishing back when Egypt, Greece and Rome were centers of civilization.

Ellis Newman, already a distinguished Catskill fisherman and flytier at the time of his early death a decade ago, made handlining both an art and science. At sportsmen's shows, Ellis, dispensing with a rod entirely, and with his right arm only, would cast as far and as accurately as most of us with a perfectly balanced rod.

In my own worm-fishing days and later in wet-fly fishing, a level line did all that was asked of it. Like most dry-fly fishermen, I now consider a tapered line a necessity.

The tapered fly line is deeply rooted in brown trout angling history—at least sport fishing in England. Half a

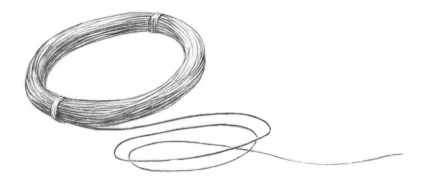

century before Columbus came to the New World, Juliana Berners was making tapered lines of horsehair—from white stallions only—varying the number of strands to suit the species. Twelve strands was the number for "great trout." Dame Juliana added a feature which I'm surprised line makers have not adopted: dyeing her lines a special color for each month of the fishing season.

Captain Terry B. Thomas, British fishing authority, fills me in on some fly-line background. In part, he reports: "Horsehair was a surprisingly good material, being strong, more or less rot-proof and when wet reasonably heavy and capable of allowing a fly to be cast.

"Around 1870, anglers started to experiment with other materials—flax, cotton, silk and a mixture of these. Silk was found to be the best material."

So, by the time the brown trout was established in American waters, a suitable line for taking *Salmo trutta* on a floating fly was ready and waiting for it.

But what a chore a silk line was—dressing it before use and during use and carefully drying it after use. In the 1930s when I was living at Lake Placid, I recall vividly that the back seat of every car parked along the West Branch of the Ausable was filled with silk lines on their drying racks.

What a blessing the modern nylon line is to the dry-fly fisherman.

The fishhook is the oldest and most stable part of fishermen's equipment. Modern patterns are strikingly similar to the bone hooks of the Stone Age dating back over five thousand years.

From the viewpoint of sport fishing for brown trout, Juliana Berners, long before her treatise was published, made her own hooks at the Abbey of St. Albans. Stealing down the backstairs to the charcoal fire, banked for the night, she would insert a square needle into the cherry-red heart of the fire until the needle glowed; then split the eye into a bend with a barb.

Professional flytiers get quite picky about fishhooks, knowing their product is sometimes judged more by the performance of the hook than the artistry of the tying job. Few experiences are more exasperating to a dry-fly angler than to lose a solid trout because the

EARLY FISH HOOKS

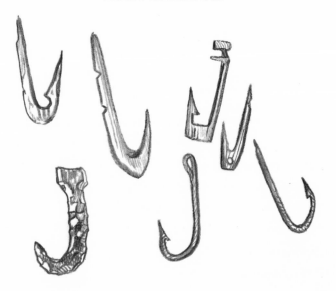

hook of a perfectly cast fly straightened out in the middle of the contest.

Of the dozen or so hook types on the market, fly-tiers narrow their choices to two or three patterns. Terry Paloot, U.S. representative of O. Mustad & Son, Norway, probably the most famous name in the fishhook world, informs me that the bulk of orders from flytiers call for a forged, hollow-point hook, bronzed, straight, round bend with a turned-down tapered eye.

FLY STYLES

Standardwing   Fanwing   Hairwing   Spentwing   Variant

Although the dry-fly fisherman may pay little attention to the hook itself, he is keenly and constantly aware of what surrounds the hook. From the moment a fisherman arrives at the stream's edge, he starts to concentrate on the best fly to use.

Are there natural flies to imitate? If not, what fly of dozens of patterns to select for an opener? As casting begins, the fly is still the center of attention. Is it turning over properly on the back cast and forward cast? Is it cocking correctly as it drops on the water? Is it reacting naturally in the currents? Is it picking up floating debris or algae? Ad infinitum. Are all these insistencies a chore? A bore? To the contrary. Selecting the right fly for the finicky brown is a challenge—part of dry-fly fishing's fascination, a fascination which makes the game both a participant sport and a spectator sport.

Roderick L. Haig-Brown[40] made an on-target cast when he declared: "It is a waste of pleasure to catch fish on a sunk fly when they can be taken on a floater."

In America, dry-fly fishermen owe Frederic Halford a special debt of gratitude. It was through Halford's writings that Theodore Gordon learned about dry-fly angling for brown trout in the chalk streams of England. A subject of growing interest to Gordon at his Neversink River base where the recently introduced brown trout was becoming well established.

The year 1890 was a landmark occasion in the history of dry-fly fishing in America. Gordon and Halford had started to correspond, and that year Halford sent Gordon a packet of four dozen dry flies, favorite patterns of British anglers.

With Halford's samples serving as prototypes, Gordon refashioned many patterns to resemble the species—mostly mayflies—found in the fast-water streams of the Catskills.

Halford became known as the father of dry-fly angling in England. Later, Theodore Gordon earned the same title in America.

But it was the brown trout in both countries that put dry-fly angling into permanent orbit.

A few years after Theodore Gordon settled in the Catskills, he was often joined on the stream and at the flytying bench by Roy Steenrod. Roy, on his own, and with coaching from Gordon, became an accomplished flytier.

After Gordon's death in 1915, Roy became the dean of what is known as the Catskill School of Flytiers, whose roster includes, besides Gordon and Steenrod, such significant names as Reuben Cross, Edward Hewitt, Herman Christian, Art Flick, Ray Smith, Ellis Newman and the two famous husband-wife teams: Walt and

Winnie Dette and Harry and Elsie Darbee. And many other fine tiers who did not become as well known.

Both Gordon and Steenrod were stout defenders of the "match-the-hatch" faith, and copied many imitations of flies captured on the Neversink, Willowemoc and Beaver Kill.

The most universally known of Gordon's creations is the Quill Gordon, or "QG," as Gordon called the fly.

"Gordon never split the wings on this fly," Roy told me, "but tied them straight up over the body. When he first tied this fly he used barbs from a wood-duck feather for tails. Later he changed to hackle barbs as he thought they took up less water.

"In attempts to imitate naturals, Gordon and I tied dozens of different patterns, but it didn't occur to us to give them all names."

Roy Steenrod originated the Hendrickson, a pattern almost as well known as the Quill Gordon. Albert E. Hendrickson, always "A. E." to Roy, was a customer of Gordon's. After Gordon's death, Hendrickson came to Roy for flies and they became fishing companions.

Driving along the Beaver Kill with Roy Steenrod a few years ago, I learned about the origin of the Hendrickson. As we passed Ferdons Pool, Roy mused: "That's where I tied my first Hendrickson. I was fishing with A. E. A terrific hatch came on and the browns began to feed furiously. I captured a few naturals and tied some imitations as best I could."

Roy's best did it. The Hendrickson, which Roy named for his friend, has remained a most successful brown trout taker since it was created that day in 1916.

The natural is the mayfly *Ephemerella subvaria*, a favorite on the brown trout's menu. Fly fishermen probably get more mileage out of *Ephemerella* than any other mayfly. The Hendrickson is the female dun; the male dun is the Red Quill, the name of an English fly, but in its Catskill version originated by Art Flick in 1933.

The female spinner becomes the Lady Beaverkill, first tied by George Cooper, another member of the Catskill School of Flytiers. In recent years, the larval form has been imitated—if you have sufficient imagination—and called the Hendrickson Nymph.

The Light Cahill—the dun of *Stenonema canadensis*—is probably better known and more widely used in the quest of brown trout than any other pattern of dry fly. Far back in flytying history a Dublin flytier gave his name to a fly of an entirely different pattern. In Irish storytelling style, Cahill's flies were said to be so lifelike that anglers would hold them to their ears thinking they might hear them buzz. At one time, I was led to believe, Dan Cahill, a brakeman on the Erie Railroad and a sometime Catskill fisherman, invented the modern version of the fly. Theodore Gordon's name has also been linked with the origin of the Light Cahill.

Roy Steenrod, today past ninety, knew both Gordon and Chandler well, and he told me: "I think the credit should go to William Chandler." Chandler, another not-so-well-known member of the Catskill coterie of flytiers, was a neighbor of Gordon's on the Neversink, as were Rube Cross and Edward Hewitt.

In the dialogue of brown trout fishermen some dry flies are known as "deceivers"—impressionistic attempts to imitate naturals. Other flies called "attractors" are more exotic creations bearing but slight resemblance to natural insects.

One of the most seductive of the attractors, the Fanwing Royal Coachman, was also Catskill-born. In 1917, Hiram Leonard, the rod maker, Thomas Mills of Mills and Son, oldest (1822) fishing-tackle shop in the United States, and Mills' son, Chester, were tackle-testing on the Esopus, perhaps the most exacting proving ground of all Catskill streams.

Stephen Mills, present head of the Mills firm, recalls the story as told to him by his father, Arthur Mills:

"After a hard day's fishing the group was relaxing in the lobby of the Kinkaid House in Phoenicia, trout capital of the Catskills at the time. During a post-mortem of the day's fishing, the talk got around to the new fly patterns of the day. In the middle of the discussion, the two Millses suddenly left, muttering something about a new idea. Soon they returned to the lobby with a new pattern—the Fanwing Royal Coachman."

Another dry fly with a Catskill cachet is the Coffin Fly, developed by Walt Dette and the late Ted Townsend, another fellow worker of mine in the State Conservation Department. The Coffin Fly is an imitation of the male spinner of *Ephemera guttulata;* its funereal black-and-white markings accounting for its name. The female dun of the species is represented by the Green Drake, the natural fly, probably the most readily recognized member of the mayfly family by fly fishermen.

Walt Dette notes that in England the male spinner is the Death Drake. "I'd never make any claims for originating a fly," says Walt. "Every time I think I've tied something new I find out, sooner or later, that it's been done before."

As a former Catskill boy, I'm loyal to the Catskill School. My fly box always contains a good supply of the Catskill traditionals: Quill Gordons, Light Cahills and Hendricksons. Since I opt for these patterns so often, their success ratio is high. But my log reveals some other fine brown-trout takers. The White Wulff, for instance. In fact, the White Wulff permits me to take more trout than my talent deserves. At evening-rise time, this fly is a satisfactory substitute for a Pale Evening Dun, although not as effective as Art Flick's gossamer Cream Variant.

Partial to the hair-wing persuasion, I've tested the White Wulff against a Royal Wulff for twenty years or more, and unlike most of my fishing friends, find the White Wulff more effective.

Checking log figures, I'm somewhat surprised to find how high on the best-taker list is the Rat Faced McDougall, another Catskill exotic with an uninhibited motif. I have an uneasy feeling my log figures are somewhat less than statistically valid. Actually it merely shows I catch the most trout on the flies I fish the most.

The Rat Faced McDougall is the brainchild of Harry Darbee[41] and the late Percy Jennings, a devoted Catskill angler. Its prototype was the Straw May, one of a series of special mayfly patterns. The series became known as the Beaverkill Bastards, listed with other long-shank, clipped, deerhair bodies in the Darbees' 1935 catalogue. A young girl friend of Jennings' daughter said the fly had personality and suggested the name.

"Why the Rat Faced McDougall should be so successful," questions Harry, "is beyond me. They don't look much like anything a trout is apt to see. However, I am not about to quarrel with success."

As dry-fly fishing fanned out from its Catskill fountainhead to other brown trout streams across the country, the traditional flies of the Catskill School—Quill Gordon, Hendrickson and Light Cahill—went along with it.

As Walt Dette once said to me: "If a dry-fly man fishing for browns doesn't have a supply of these flies with him, he feels he's fishing naked."

The same species of mayflies hatching in the same streams year after year give the dry-fly fishing world a stability seldom found in these times.

Dan Holland,[42] former Fishing Editor of *Field & Stream*—he bought my first fishing story back in 1939—reminds dry-fly anglers of the old adage: "When the leaf of the elm is as big as a squirrel's ear, the trout will rise to a floating fly."

This is a signal for the Eastern dry-fly angler to inaugurate the season, as Catskill anglers do, with the Quill Gordon, followed shortly with the Hendrickson and then by the Light Cahill.

Dan Bailey, renowned Western flytier and fly fisherman, an Eastern expatriate and former Catskill angler now based in Livingston, Montana, writes: "I take the Quill Gordon and Light Cahill on practically every fishing trip. These two, with the Hendrickson, I would certainly list in my top six dry flies if not higher." Dan also lists the Royal Wulff, Goofus Bug, Joe's Hopper and Adams. The last, of Michigan lineage, is also high on my list. My log shows the Adams to be a brown-trout taker with a success pedigree that challenges the original Catskill trio.

The fly is certainly the most intriguing piece of the dry-fly fisherman's tackle, but the rod, the reel and the line also offer countless permutations, permitting the angler a wide range of individual preferences.

Indeed, the tools of the trade, tuned to the brown trout's wiles, in the hands of a dry-fly angler combine delightfully in a harmoniously orchestrated performance.

Tactics

To match the wiles of *Salmo trutta*, a dry-fly fisherman needs a special strategy. In my own confrontations, the brown trout is far ahead in the scoring. Yet, despite more than half a century of coming off second best, my enthusiasm for the contest and the brown trout as an adversary remains undiminished.

This gung-ho yen was always a puzzle to my parents. I like to think I am a throwback to my tweedy English ancestry, to a great-uncle from the classic chalk-stream country of Hampshire.

A British sporting journal, in 1896, reported: "He was a fine angler. He would dispatch his dry fly upon almost impossible errands and fetch the 2- and 3-pound trout from under the farthest banks of the pretty Hornbridge portion of the Test."

Long ago, I realized I would never be able to reach such proficiency. Snubbed by *Salmo trutta* like a door-to-door salesman, a dogged persistence helps offset the poor casting habits of a lifetime of fishing, now perma-pressed into my reflexes.

Ellis Newman, the Catskill flytier and one of the country's top casting experts, was determined to make me an accomplished double-haul caster. But Ellis, a natural-born teacher, after years of trying, finally had to flunk me.

But I am convinced that brown trout can be caught with ideas as well as Quill Gordons. This approach—enthusiasm for the quarry, persistence and ideas—keeps paying dividends. I call this approach "streammanship." Streammanship starts at streamside. Long ago, Confucius pointed out that proper preparation is invariably the seed of success.

In my early dry-fly fishing days, I would set up shop at my car, rush to the stream and begin whipping the water to a froth. Recently restructuring my opening gambit, I rig up at streamside. From a concealed observation post, I keep an eye open for bulletins: rises, ripples, rings, dimples, boils, bubbles, bulges, swirls. Flies—hatching or hovering. Sunshine and shadows.

This kind of monitoring does not always yield clues, but sometimes a snippet of action is a tip which

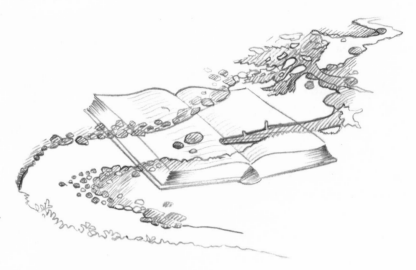

brings a prompt pay-off. One trout in the creel and hoping for an encore! That's the way to begin a day's fishing.

I am so indebted to many accredited masters who have gone before me that I would like to share with to-day's anglers my own translation of a cross-pollination of tips of the trade—streammanship ideas which have helped me in the uneven match with the brown trout.

Back at the stream. If rises are spotted, mobilizing for action is simplified. Frequently the fly which is hatching can be identified so a facsimile can be selected. If not, at least it can be determined whether to use a light or dark-colored fly.

Next, I try to get a good fix on the location of the rise. If several trout are rising, one fish must be selected, just as the waterfowl gunner selects one duck from a passing flock.

The throw should be well above the ring of the rise. A brown often follows down under the fly for several yards before coming to the surface to take it.

Timing is essential, too. The rhythm of casting should match the rhythm of the rise. For most of us, this simply requires a slowdown in the lockstep style of casting almost universally adopted by American dry-fly fishermen. Sufficient time should be allowed for a brown trout to return to its regular feeding position. A slapdash, poorly directed cast at this time is disastrous. It will put a feeding trout down as surely as line overrun will cause a backlash.

In orthodox upstream-and-across dry-fly fishing, cross-currents—sometimes the fly changes lanes like a turnpike hot-rodder—make it difficult or impossible to cast without encountering drag. In these situations, I anchor myself in the stream in a straight line well below the rising trout, remembering to throw the fly well above the rise.

In fast water it is also almost impossible to retrieve the slack line quickly enough to keep it under control. Speeding downstream in a beeline directly at me, the fly catches the seat of my waders more often than a trout. But a drag-free float is worth the many times I flub it.

If there are no signals coming from the water when I start a day's fishing, I fish the water instead of the rise. "Fishing on spec," Theodore Gordon called it.

A right-handed caster, I usually work up the left side of a stream. I find most of my favorite streams have three major threads of current: a current on my side where I cast first; a middle current which gets my attention next; and one on the far side where I finish up on a stretch.

Sometimes I hook a trout on the near side and if there is not too much flummoxing around, I find another, present and voting, in one of the other currents. I am waiting for the day when the system pays off in a three-trout parlay.

On those rare days when the proportion of takes to

rises is like red coming up two times out of three on the wheel, I think I have cracked the code. But on the very next trip, *Salmo trutta*, as unpredictable as it is wily, puts me back in my place. Frustration, exasperation and humiliation take over—usually in that order.

Dry-fly fishermen continually debate whether to cast to the head or tail of a pool first. Most often I start at the lower end of the pool and work up. On a few lucky occasions I have taken a trout in the tail end of the pool and enjoyed an instant replay farther up.

However, on pools where I know a float can be completed through its entire length, I start casting to the head of the pool. To avoid dunking the fly, I drop it just below the tasseled waterfall where the water enters from the pool above.

Ray Smith, Catskill flytier, who is to the Esopus what Art Flick is to the Schoharie, is another angling ombudsman of mine. He made me a true believer in the long float.

Ray, although well aware of the disastrous effects of drag, convinced me I could get more mileage out of every cast.

"Let your fly finish its float even if drag takes it under—unless, of course, it snags."

For me, easier said than done. My internal machinery is so fabricated that I am programmed for recycling a cast the moment the fly is sucked under.

"But as long as your fly is on or in the water, you have a chance of picking up a fish," Ray points out, adding, "Besides, letting the fly finish its float means a softer pickup."

Fast-water brown trout streams are my favorite challenge. Currents literally throw me a curve. Indeed, in a trout-stream manuscript, currents are the pages I have most difficulty in reading.

A bothersome current is a devilish bugaboo. Sometimes I station myself upstream in the spot I have been casting to, watching the course of bits of wooden matches as I break them in pieces and toss them in the water. Old, worn-out flies, too—barbs and hooks cut off—occasionally perform their last service in this rite. I have learned from this what most dry-fly fishermen already know: a dry fly attached to a leader behaves in an entirely different fashion than a free-floating natural.

I keep hoping that we dry-fly anglers do not always have to be at the mercy of stream currents. I like to believe that trout-stream hydraulics, as related to dry-fly fishing, is still an untapped field of exploration. I live for the day when a hydraulic engineer who is also a keen dry-fly fisherman will do for currents what engineers have done for fly-rod dynamics.

At times, a brown trout's preference for a particular natural fly is incredible. And some of these times, it is practically impossible to tell by ordinary observation just what *Salmo trutta* is taking.

I recall such a day on New York's Roeliff Jansen Kill. The Roeliff is a marginal trout stream, a textbook example of the brown trout's ability to withstand high water temperatures and the competition of bass and pickerel. With headwaters partly in Massachusetts, the Roeliff serpentines like a mended fly line through a low-lying valley for fifty miles to the historic Hudson.

It was a sultry day in June, and across the river the Catskills loomed up in a mist-tinted mood piece right out of Washington Irving. In fact, a thunderstorm was rolling up and down Rip Van Winkle's valley as the Dutchmen bowled ninepins.

Much of the Roeliff is wide and wadeable, so I fish up the middle, covering pools and pockets in a kind of minesweeping operation.

I came into a bend with a long, glassy pool snugged into the curve, the tail of the pool showing just a trace of a ripple. There, in full view, was the largest brown trout I ever observed surface-feeding. Sixteen inches or more, sporting like a porpoise, in a perfect feeding syndrome. Slapping the water with its tail like a beaver on every rise.

I was able to put myself in perfect position well below the rings of the rise without spooking the trout. I checked the No. 12 Light Cahill I had been using, inspecting barb and point and carefully drying it. My nerves seemed surprisingly steady—this was the biggest brown in full view I had ever cast to—and I achieved a cast Ellis Newman would have approved, the fly dropping as light as a hackle feather in front of the trout just before it rose.

I was sure the fish had taken the fly. I struck hard to set the hook. The fly skidded off the water, churning a wake, whizzing past my ear.

"Dammit," I thought, "that will certainly put the fish down."

But it didn't. The big brown kept rising, its insisting rhythm unbroken. I kept casting, searching the water between casts, hoping to discover what the fish was feeding on. Sometimes a hatching fly will cling to waders at the waterline. From the trout's surface acrobatics, I was convinced the big fish was not nymphing. Sometimes it seemed as if the trout even pushed my artificial aside to take the natural.

I began to change patterns and sizes in rapid order. My nerves, I discovered, were not as steady as I thought. I was grateful I had learned an old trick of the trade. During the fishing season, I let the nails on my thumbs and forefingers grow long and clipped with a fairly straight edge—a big help in threading flies and ty-

Tactics

ing and untying knots. This Fu Manchu technique was paying off now.

I tried flies that I had been carrying in my fly box for years but never used: Tups Indispensable, White-Winged Black Gnat, Light Cahill Spider and vintage flies whose names I could not recall.

The big brown continued to be underwhelmed by my free sample program—the superb Darbee/Dette offerings suddenly invested with a devalued recognition factor.

I kept casting; the trout kept refusing. A situation which will strike a responsive chord in the heart of every dry-fly man. The supreme insult. I couldn't take the fish and I couldn't put it down.

But nature did. The storm which had been rumbling in the Catskills suddenly swept across the Hudson, bringing a torrential downpour. Soon the stream was in spate, turning the color of café au lait.

Later, I told an angling purist about the experience.

"Feeding on midges, no doubt," he said with cavalier certainty, adding with just a touch of the needle, "Like poetic license, I suppose every fishing writer is entitled to one fish that got away."

Every dry-fly fisherman has been teased by brown trout on a short-rise kick. Even more tantalizing when punctuated by a momentary take. The counterattack usually calls for a smaller fly. At times when I have a feeling the hatch may end at any moment, or at the lavender end of the evening rise, I save time by following another suggestion of Ray Smith's. I get out the scissors to fashion a smaller version of the fly I am using. The trimmed-down fly works often enough to make the haircut technique profitable. Some of these flies—seemingly the most successful—end up as sparsely dressed as a strip-teaser after the fifth round of applause.

Not infrequently a brown trout will make a pass at the line-to-leader knot—sometimes even at wind knots on the leader. Here, again, a fly tied on a small-sized hook is indicated. In fact, in the last ten years or more there has been a trend toward smaller artificials.

Speaking for dry-fly fishermen of the Esopus and other streams of the Hudson River drainage, Ray Smith told me: "The patterns have stayed pretty much the same, but smaller fish—and some say hatches of smaller flies—have created a demand for dressing the old stand-bys on smaller hooks."

"That holds true on the Beaver Kill and other streams in the Delaware Watershed," Harry Darbee reported.

Terry Paloot of Mustad, speaking of the general across-the-board increase in the sales of hooks from flytiers, confirmed the increased demand for smaller hooks, adding, "Believe it or not, I recently received a letter from a flytier who complained that No. 28 was too large and he wanted a hook in No. 32!"

All the Catskill flytiers were fishermen before they became flytiers. They are still fishermen. Ray Smith spends more time on the stream than at the tying bench. Ray is the iconoclast of the Catskill School of Flytiers. He still sticks to a stout 7½-foot leader. And, as already reported, he does not consider drag the curse it has been made out to be.

To most dry-fly men, stiff hackle is the name of the game.

"I often wonder," Ray mused, as we chatted in his shop, "what you fellows are trying to prove when you touch the hackle tips of a fly to your lips. I'll put a certain shade of color over stiff hackle every time."

The Red Fox, a consistent brown trout taker, in its Catskill version originated by Ray is dressed almost like a Light Cahill, except red belly fur instead of light belly fur of the red fox is used for the body; the hackle is a buff ginger from a Minorca or Leghorn rooster.

As Heraclitus observed: "You never swim in the same river twice," so one never fishes the same brown trout stream twice. The variables are so infinite that they are never in the same combination: year, season, month, day, stream flow, water depth, turbidity, color, air temperature, water temperature, barometric pressure, humidity, cloud cover, rainfall—even the phase of the moon, perhaps—and a myriad of other influences which determine a brown trout's preference for a particular fly at a particular time.

One of the most intriguing aspects of the dry-fly faith is looking forward to each encounter with the brown trout in a new and different frame of reference.

Seeking the brown trout via the dry fly, I have a tendency to cast in the same trade routes the same way time after time. Looking back, I feel the tips which have helped me most in my encounters with *Salmo trutta* have been garnered through a careful study of each pool/riff complex as it is approached.

However, a few successful tactics I have learned by accident. Like my "edge cast." A log jam across a narrow pool demanded an especially true cast. To check line length, I made a dry-run cast up my side of the stream. The fly dropped close to shore in water not over six inches deep. In a burst of spray, appearing as mysteriously as a wind knot on a leader, came a gee-whizz ten-incher in an acrobatic cartwheel as I shortened line. Now I always give the shallow shore sections a couple of casts as I move upstream.

Ray Smith once told me: "I've caught brown trout everywhere, so I fish for 'em everywhere."

Another accidental discovery is what I call a

"bounce cast." The stream was a boulder-studded section of my beloved Rondout. Trying to drop a fly in the cushion water close to the boulder, I made a poor cast. The fly hit the boulder and bounced into the faster water outside the cushion, bobbing around as in a Mixmaster. In a flash, an ebullient brown struck savagely, demonstrating its high octane rating for the next few minutes. Since then, I purposely throw the bounce cast, trying not only to ricochet the fly off the boulder but also to drop it into the fast water outside the quiet cushion water. Possibly this spot is also in better view from the trout's window.

Most of us also try to place a fly as close to the edge of an undercut bank as possible. Here, too, it seems logical that a fly passing the undercut a few feet out from the edge has a better chance of being in the trout's area of vision.

Years ago, I was told that brown trout prefer a position in front of a boulder. Later, as a fisheries biologist making stream population counts with an electric shocking device, I tried to find out if this was a valid premise. Without success. Mostly because when fish first feel the current, they immediately move to escape.

More recently I was told that a brown's favorite spot is in back of a boulder where the current forms a

vacuum—the "souse hole" of white-water river rafters—which pulls floating food down to make easy pickings for the waiting trout. Maybe.

In my own experience, especially in using the bounce cast, I invariably take browns along the side of the boulder, the strike being so immediate that I feel sure the fish must have been close to the rock.

I have also taken quite a few boulder-oriented browns blind-sided. Shielded by the rock, I loop the cast to drop the fly on the far side, a method with an extra bit of anticipation because I am also fishing blind-sided.

An idea gleaned from the peerless tactician George La Branche is fishing the edge of the foam—beggar's-balm in England—which piles up like the collar on lager in the backsets of slow-moving pools. A brown trout, reacting to its strong phototropic inclination, seeks the shade under the foam. La Branche also mentions taking a trout by dropping a fly into the middle of the foam patch, a feat I have yet to accomplish. The few brown trout I have taken by this tactic were outside the edge of the foam—again, I presume, more in line with the vision of the trout through its window.

In the local streams I fish regularly, I mark the brown trout I return to the water by cutting off the adipose fin. This is a carry-over from my days as a fisheries biologist when marked trout helped to check on growth and survival and—by comparing the proportion of marked to unmarked trout—an estimate of the standing population in a body of water.

Nowadays, I mark brown trout for more personal rewards. Catching a fish marked and released a year or more before is like meeting an old friend who has grown in stature during the interim and fulfilled your estimate of his potential.

In keeping book on brown trout for sixty years, there is one trout that stands out above all others in my memory—the Ledge Pool Brown.

The Ledge Pool, etched in shale rock with pencils of light piercing overhanging hemlocks, is hidden in a soul-beckoning, storybook kind of trout stream—a stream I have promised not to identify.

The Ledge Pool Brown first appeared on my angling agenda on one of those gentle May mornings full of poetic overtones of fresh colors and fragrance. A pedestrian flick of a Hendrickson brought a trout out from its cavernous home under a rock ledge. As it glistened in the swirl, I saw it was the four-to-the-pound variety. Brown trout being endowed with such a strong territorial imperative, I had expected a larger fish in such a choice spot. But I did not expect the fight it was putting up.

"Foul-hooked," I thought, impressed with its pizazz. But it was hooked in the lip. As I snipped off the adipose fin, admiring its bright golden luster shining like a freshly minted coin, I again wondered how such a small trout could hold its position against bigger trout. It was a tip-off that the Ledge Pool Brown was no ordinary trout.

Several times during the season I returned to the pool but could not raise the fish. I began to suspect that it had been driven out by a larger, more aggressive trout.

Early the next season I was back at the stream to test the appetite of the Ledge Pool Brown. The trout rose on the second cast. A Hendrickson again. A smashing strike showed the fish was even more combat-oriented than before. Most brown trout, I have discovered, head downstream when first hooked. The Ledge Pool Brown made a short dash upstream, breaking the leader on the sharp edge of the ledge. Thinking things over later, I realized that if I was ever to take this trout, I would have to check it on its first rush to keep the leader from being snapped.

Later, I returned to the Ledge Pool, my strategy well fixed in mind. But the Ledge Pool Brown would not come out of its precinct.

There's nothing like rain to tickle up a trout stream during dog-day doldrums. One time during the summer, I made a pit stop at the Ledge Pool after a shower but the trout refused all offerings. When a stream has a slight roil, I have found that a White Wulff or a Rat Faced MacDougall frequently stir up interest, but even these old standbys failed.

Another time, after a gentle rain which did not discolor the stream, I tried the Ledge Pool. On one cast I thought I spotted an investigative flash—like a subliminal advertisement in a TV commercial. Sometimes this is a clue to an angler that he has a chance to make a sale.

So I stood as still as a great blue heron for a long time before casting again. But the Ledge Pool Brown ignored all my offerings.

The next season I was not able to get to the Ledge Pool until late May. I viewed the scene with dismay. A windfall below the pool left no room for the backcast of a right-handed caster. There were no options for a dry-fly man. Unless I stooped to a downstream roll cast it had to be a backhand cast over the left shoulder. And the backcast had to be kept low, a foot or two above the water. As every fly fisherman knows, a low backcast is a sure way to malfunction.

I tied on a Hendrickson again and let go. I could feel the hit right down to the cork grip. The Ledge Pool Brown headed upstream for the sharp edge of the ledge.

I held firm. So did the tackle. A testimonial to the 5X leader and the little two-ounce Orvis rod—bent in an arc, the tip a couple of feet from the grip.

Unable to reach the ledge, the trout suddenly turned and headed straight toward me, piling up an alarming amount of slack at my feet.

Then, with show-biz flair for the dramatic, the trout made a 90-degree turn, heading downstream. Splashing and stumbling on the jagged rocks, I was led down two pools. Once, slipping to my knees, I shipped a little water. Don Quixote's truism flashed in my mind: "There's no taking trout with dry breeches."

Now I managed to snug up the slack and, under my auspices, finessed the trout down to a larger pool. It made a lightning-fast swing around the pool, apparently casing it for an escape route. I was five minutes into the transaction with no signs of a let-up on the part of the fish.

Next it found a hollow under a flat stone where it sulked. I pressed my luck, increasing the tension on the line. Suddenly, still highly motivated for escape, the trout came out from under the stone, leaping clear of the water with a savage shake of its head, trying to dislodge the hook. Feinting an upstream dash, it reversed its field, heading downstream at full throttle intent on reaching the pool below. Again I tested the leader and rod, just barely keeping the trout from sliding over the lip of the pool.

I sensed this was the turning point. Back in the pool, the fish whipsawed back and forth with reduced vigor but still with gallant élan.

Next, a nice bit of point counterpoint as I gave out and took in line. A power dive to the bottom and a barrel roll, ending with the trout listing to starboard.

A moment later, the fish was cashiered on the

shore. Dark bronze with the patina of age, heavy-shouldered and deep-bellied with a hook beginning to form on its lower jaw—and a small bump where the adipose fin used to be—the magnificent Ledge Pool Brown.

It is moments like these which are forever creeled in the memory of an angler. It is moments like these which help to explain the rationale of dry-fly fishing for brown trout; which reveal the attention a dry-fly angler applies to tactics he hopes will match the cunning of his quarry. It is moments like these which unveil the subtle chemistry between the brown trout and the dry-fly fisherman; which underscore the wonderful and enduring charisma of *Salmo trutta.*

The strategy of the dry-fly angler, pitted against the brown trout, has been developing for more than five centuries. Tactics for catching the brown have one basic premise: to make the confrontations between angler and trout more even.

In deciphering the countless variables in the drama, many yet to be discovered, defined and analyzed, a big gap looms between angling rhetoric and angling success.

The brown trout, too, rugged resistance the most constant element in its own tactics, has grown more canny, still springing new stratagems to keep *Salmo trutta* the most challenging quarry.

Dry-fly fishing for the brown trout is more than a sport. It is a branch of philosophy.

Last Cast

The brown trout has given me some of my finest hours: hours of work and recreation in nature's loveliest settings; hours in college classrooms, academic disciplines helping me to understand what makes the brown trout tick; hours in a trout hatchery, rubbing shoulders with disciples of Fred Mather, who first introduced the brown trout to America; hours in the field as a fisheries biologist, investigating, analyzing, evaluating the brown's ecological relationships in such classic environments as the Neversink and Beaver Kill; hours as an administrator, collaborating on policy and management decisions which determined the quality of brown trout fishing for thousands of anglers; hours at a desk as a writer, trying to recapture in words the way *Salmo trutta* creates the best of all angling worlds.

A deep-seated wanderlust, an amazing adaptability and a strong survival instinct made *Salmo trutta*, in both its native habitat and its adopted range, the universal sporting fish.

With a heritage whose years are measured in millions, the brown trout has grown in stature as a game fish since the days of Claudius Aelianus, its personality and character dominating the angling scene more with each passing fishing season. In this topsy-turvy world of distortions and devaluations, I find the sturdy, steadfast brown trout brings a welcome stability to my life.

And the inspiring qualities of the brown trout bring out the best in man. The ideal fish deserves the ideal angler. Far from the contemptuous eyes of the cynics, the angler, alone on the stream, adds a new dimension to his sport as he meets his quarry with a self-imposed code of conduct.

After a few encounters with the new resident on the Neversink, Theodore Gordon, who cut his angling teeth on brook trout, was won over to the brown. "The brown trout is a noble game fish," he declared, "which affords a man a sensation he is in no danger of forgetting to the last day of his life."

For me, *Salmo trutta* still strikes the same responsive chords as the day in 1910 I caught my first brown trout in the Catskill's Rondout: the challenge of a worthy adversary; the perfect float of a fly to an avid surface feeder; the characteristic swirl and burst of spray; the distinctive savage rush and sudden tug as the line tightens. All these mighty moments. And more: the witchery, peace and beauty; the reveries that transform a brown trout stream into a perfect poem—the pure absolutes, as Plato taught, which lie beyond objective reality.

Fortune continues to smile on me since that unforgettable day on the Rondout. *Salmo trutta* still holds its original franchise on my affections.

For one so firmly hooked, there is a temptation to linger over a farewell to the noble fish. An entire book, with such a pretentious title, devoted to one species of fish, might lead one to assume that everything is known about *Salmo trutta.* But it soon becomes obvious that there is still much to be learned about this complicated creature.

So, speaking for the brotherhood, I say hail—but not farewell—to the brown trout, a fabulous fish bringing joy to the heart, solace to the spirit and enrichment to life.

Acknowledgments

As unsatisfactory as a soggy Fanwing, acknowledgment is a poor word to express my debt to the scores of individuals who guided me in compiling the brown trout story.

Actually, *The Compleat Brown Trout* is a testimonial to countless professional colleagues and fishermen, far and near, whose knowledge, skills and experience shine through so many pages. Many, I regret, go unrecognized but not unthanked.

It will come as no surprise to the friends of the ubiquitous Sparse Grey Hackle to learn he had a helping hand in getting me started on the brown trout saga. Almost two decades ago, his casts in my behalf to the editors of *Sports Illustrated* brought a rise which resulted in an article, "The Brown Trout: A Success Story" (April 30, 1956). Mr. Hackle, however, should not be held responsible for subsequent shortcomings of his protégé.

Worldwide research brought in so much more material than could be used in a short piece that my wife said, "Someday you should do a book on the critter."

That someday has arrived. Through Dottie's encouragement I got started, and through her help I finished it.

I am grateful to many former professional colleagues in the New York State Conservation Department, especially Dr. U. B. Stone, Neil Ehlinger and Earl Harris for supplying and checking certain factual material. And to Roy Steenrod, longtime fellow worker and a companion on far too few fishing trips, for his remarkable recall of the golden age of brown trout fishing in the Catskills. And to Ray Smith, Catskill fisherman and flytier, another angling mentor, for no-nonsense practical tips. And finally to Dr. John F. Vuilleumier, Swiss writer, a friend for fifty years who, on the occasion of my eighteenth birthday, opened up the wonderful world of angling literature with a gift of Alfred Ronald's "The Fly-Fisher's Entomology."

I thank colleagues throughout the United States for a phenomenal response to my inquiry about the original introduction of brown trout. So prevailing is the brotherhood spirit in the profession that the canvass produced replies from all fifty states!

I am indebted to Dr. K. E. Banister of the British

Museum (Natural History) for assistance in checking scientific literature and making it possible to inspect preserved specimens of numerous racial strains of brown trout in the Museum's extensive collection. Also to Dr. W. E. Frost and Dr. M. E. Brown, authors of *The Trout* (London, Collins, 1967) for gathering in one volume much up-to-date information to complement the vintage notes of Dr. George C. Embody, and other professors, taken as a graduate student at Cornell University. *The Trout* also helped to stimulate my thinking in planning the format of my chronicle.

I also thank Commander O. S. M. Bayley, Hon. Secretary of the Salmon and Trout Association, for making it possible to use the Association's library in its headquarters at Fishmonger's Hall, London, and especially for personally selecting many appropriate books for me to inspect.

To local libraries—Millbrook Library and Mid-Hudson Library—my appreciation for obtaining many hard-to-get references needed to hew as close to the book's title as my capability permits.

I have recycled some concepts and rewoven threads of material from articles of mine that appeared in *Outdoor Life* ("The Charmed Circle of the Catskills," March 1969; "The Charmed Circle Completed," April 1969; "The Catskill Flytiers," May 1972; "Never Too Late," April 1973) and *Field & Stream* ("The ABC of Trout Fishing," August 1939; "Bamboo Aristocrats," February 1958). The editors of these magazines have kindly permitted me to use the material.

And, finally, my thanks to the fabulous fish, itself, which made this book such a labor of love.

Bibliography

TEXT REFERENCES

1. Claudius Aelianus. *De Animalium Natura.* A.D. 230 Tiguri, apud Gesneros fratres, 1556. And other editions.
2. Dame Juliana Berners. *A Treatyse of Fysshynge wyth an Angle.* First printed in the *Boke of St. Albans* (second edition). Westminster, 1496. And other editions.
3. Leonard Mascall. *A Book of Fishing with Hooke and Line.* London, 1590.
4. Gervase Markham. *A Discourse of the Generall Art of Fishing.* First printed in *The Second Book of the English Husbandman.* London, 1614. And other editions.

5. William Lawson. *A New Orchard and Garden.* London, 1617–18. And other editions.

6. Thomas Barker. *The Art of Angling.* London, 1651. And other editions.

7. John Dennys. *The Secrets of Angling.* London, 1613. And other editions.

8. Izaak Walton. *The Compleat Angler.* London, 1653. And 384 other editions as of 1967.

9. George P. R. Pulman. *Vade Mecum of Fly-fishing for Trout.* London and Axminster, 1841. Second edition, 1846. Third edition, 1851.

10. Frederic M. Halford. *Floating Flies and How to Tie Them.* London, 1886. And other editions.
———. *Dry Fly Fishing in Theory and Practice.* London, 1889. And other editions.
———. *Dry Fly Entomology.* London, 1897. And other editions.
———. *Modern Development of the Dry Fly.* London, 1910.

11. George M. L. La Branche. *The Dry Fly and Fast Water.* New York, Scribner, 1914.

12. John McDonald. *The Complete Fly Fisherman.* The notes and letters of Theodore Gordon. New York, Scribner, 1947.

13. Colin Fletcher. "Brown Trout Around the World." *The Fisherman,* August 1958.

14. Hugh R. MacCrimmon and T. L. Marshall. "World Distribution of Brown Trout, *Salmo trutta.*" *Journal Fisheries Research Board, Canada,* 25, 1968.
———, ———, and Barra L. Gots. "World Distribution of Brown Trout, *Salmo trutta:* Further Observations," *Journal Fisheries Research Board, Canada,* 27, 1970.

15. James Westman. *Why Fish Bite and Why They Don't.* Englewood Cliffs, N.J., Prentice-Hall, 1961.

16. Carl Linnaeus. *Systema Naturae.* 1758.

17. A. C. L. G. Günther. *Catalogue of the Fishes of the British Museum,* Vol. 6. 1866.

18. Francis Day. *British and Irish Salmonidae.* London, Williams & Norgate, 1887.

19. C. Tate Regan. *The Freshwater Fishes of the British Isles.* London, Methuen, 1911.

20. L. S. Berg. *Poissons de L'URSS.* Leningrad, 1932.

21. E. Trewavas. "Sea Trout and Brown Trout." *The Salmon and Trout Magazine* (London), September 1953.

22. J. Schmidt. "Racial Investigations." *C. R. Laboratory Carlsberg,* 14, 1921.

23. A. V. Tåning. "Experimental Study of Meristic Characters in Fishes. *Biological Review Cambridge*, 27, 1952.

24. Frank W. Law, M.D., F.R.C.S. "The Fish's Point of View." *The Salmon and Trout Magazine* (London), January 1968.

25. Gordon L. Walls. "The Vertebrate Eye." *Cranbrook Institute of Science Bulletin*, No. 19, August 1942.

26. John R. Greeley. "The Spawning Habits of Brook, Brown and Rainbow Trout and the Problem of Egg Predators." *Transactions, American Fisheries Society*, 1932.

27. W. E. Frost and M. E. Brown. *The Trout*. London and Glasgow, Collins, 1967.

28. Charles R. Deuel, David C. Haskell, and A. V. Tunison. *The New York State Fish Hatchery Feeding Chart*. Albany, New York State Conservation Department, 1937. Revised 1942, 1952.

29. James G. Needham and Paul R. Needham. *A Guide to the Study of Fresh-Water Biology*. Ithaca and New York, Comstock, 1938. And revised editions.

30. Alfred Ronalds. *The Fly-Fisher's Entomology*. London, 1836. And other editions.

31. Preston J. Jennings. *A Book of Trout Flies*. New York, Crown, 1935.

32. Charles M. Wetzel. *Practical Fly Fishing*. Boston, Christopher, 1943.

33. Arthur B. Flick. *Streamside Guide to Naturals and Their Imitations*. New York, Putnam, 1947.
    ———. *Art Flick's New Streamside Guide to Naturals and Their Imitations*. New York, Crown, 1969.

34. Paul R. Needham. *Trout Streams*. Ithaca and New York, Comstock, 1938. Revised by Prof. Carl E. Bond: New York, Winchester, 1969.

35. Edward R. Hewitt. *Handbook of Stream Improvement*. New York, Marchbanks, 1934.

36. Carl L. Hubbs, J. R. Greeley, and Clarence M. Tarzwell. "Methods for the Improvement of Michigan Trout Streams." *Bulletin No. 1, Institute of Fisheries Research*. Ann Arbor, Mich., 1932.

37. Eugene V. Connett. *My Friend the Trout*. New York, D. Van Nostrand, 1961.
    ———. *Any Luck?* Garden City, N.Y., Windward House, 1937.

38. Alvin R. Grove, Jr. *The Lure and Lore of Trout Fishing*. Harrisburg, Pa., Stackpole, 1951. Reprint: Rockville Centre, N.Y., Freshet no date.

39. Charles Ritz. *A Fly Fisher's Life*. London, Max Reinhart, 1959; New York, Winchester, 1969.

40. Roderick L. Haig-Brown. *Fisherman's Spring.* New York, William Morrow, 1951.

41. Harry Darbee. "The Two-Fathered Fly," from *The Gordon Garland.* Published for subscribers by the Theodore Gordon Flyfishers, New York, 1965.

42. Dan Holland. *The Trout Fisherman's Bible.* Garden City, N.Y., Doubleday, 1949.

ADDITIONAL REFERENCES

Brown, M. E. *The Physiology of Fishes:* Vol. 1, *Metabolism,* Vol. 2, *Behavior.* New York, Academic Press, 1951.

Brynildson, Oscar M., Hacker, Vernon A., and Klick, Thomas A. *Brown Trout: Its Life History, Ecology and Management.* Madison, Wis., Wisconsin Conservation Department, Publication 234, 1964.

Calderwood, W. L. *Salmon and Sea Trout.* London, Edward Arnold, 1930.

Cornell, J. H. "The Brown Trout." *Wildlife in North Carolina,* March 1971.

Curtis, Brian. *The Life Story of the Fish.* New York, Harcourt, 1949. Revised edition: New York, Dover, 1961.

Dahl, K. "Are Brown and Sea Trout Interchangeable?" *The Salmon and Trout Magazine* (London), June 1933.

Fenderson, Carll N. *The Brown Trout in Maine.* Augusta, Maine Department of Inland Fisheries and Game, 1954.

Gill, Emlyn M. *Practical Dry-Fly Fishing.* New York, Scribner, 1913.

Harding, Col. E. W. *The Trout's Point of View.* London, Seeley Service, 1931.

Hills, John Waller. *A History of Fly Fishing for Trout.* London, Philip Allen, 1921. And other editions.

Hobbs, Derisley F. "Trout Fisheries in New Zealand." *Fisheries Bulletin No. 9.* New Zealand Marine Department, Wellington, N. Z., 1948.

Lamond, Henry. *The Sea Trout.* London, Sherrat and Hughes, 1916.

Malloch, P. D. *Life History and Habits of the Salmon, Sea Trout and Other Freshwater Fish.* London, Adam and Charles Black, 1910.

Marinaro, Vincent. *A Modern Dry-Fly Code.* New York, Putnam, 1950. And other editions.

McClane, A. J. "Brown Trout." *Field & Stream,* December 1971.

Menzies, W. J. M. *Sea Trout and Trout.* London, Edward Arnold, 1936.

Mills, Derek. *Salmon and Trout: A Resource, Its Ecology, Conservation and Management.* Edinburgh, Oliver & Boyd, 1971.

Nall, G. Herbert. *The Life of the Sea Trout.* London, Seeley Service, 1930.

Pyefinch, K. A. *Trout in Scotland.* Edinburgh, H. M. Stationery Office, 1960.

Schwiebert, Ernest G. *Matching the Hatch.* New York, Macmillan, 1955.

Skues, G. E. M. *The Way of a Trout with a Fly.* London, Adam and Charles Black, 1921.

Van Someren, V. D. *The Biology of Trout in Kenya Colony.* Nairobi, Government Printer, 1952.

173

Bibliography

Index

Aberdare Mountains, Africa, trout streams in, 14
acid-alkaline content of water in trout streams, 121–22
Ackley, Professor H.S., 82
Aelianus, Claudius, 3, 23, 162
Africa, introduction of brown trout in, 13–15
age of trout, calculating from scale annuli *(chart and drawing)*, 76–77

aging, natural, of bodies of water, 122–23
Ainsworth, Stephen, 82
air bladder, function of, 42–43
"algae blooms," 123
America, introduction of brown trout in, 5, 15–23
American Fisheries Society, 21
anatomy, *see* body structure of brown trout
Annin, Harry, 84

Arkansas River, Colorado, 115

"attractors" (dry flies), 140–41

Ausable River, Michigan, 5, 82

Ausable River (West Branch),
New York, 93, 115, 123

Australia, introduction of
brown trout in, 12

bacterial infections, 89

Bailey, Dan, 143

Barker, Thomas, 3

bass, 103, 124–25

Batten Kill, Vermont, 5

Beaver Kill, New York, 5, 24,
67, 73, 95, 112, 113, 121,
122, 128, 139, 153, 162

Bedford, Duke of, 15

Berg, L.S., 33 *and n.*

Berners, Juliana, 3, 4, 98, 130,
135, 136

blood system in trout, 38

body structure of brown trout,
25–27 *ff.; diagram of,* 26
See also skeleton

books on trout and fishing,
3–4, 5

"bounce cast," 155

British Museum, fish specimens in, 32

Brodheads River, Pennsylvania, 5

brook trout, 19–20, 30, 31, 82,
83, 103, 120

Brown, Dr. M.E., 68

Buckland, Frank, 12

bullheads, 60

"Bull-trout," 30

Bushmans River, Natal, 13

business, fishing and fishermen as a market in, 3

caddis flies, 95, 98; *chart,* 99

Cahill, Dan, 140

Canada, brown trout in, 17,
21–22

casting, 137; techniques of,
analyzed, 146–48, 158; *diagram of,* 131

cataracts, eye, in trout, 89

Catskill Mountains, trout
streams in, 5, 112, 122,
128, 129, 130, 134, 138,
139

Catskill School of Flytiers, 5,
130, 134, 138, 140, 141

"catch and release" fishing,
113, 115

Chandler, William, 140

characteristics of brown trout,
2, 7–8, 97, 151, 155–56
See also phototropism *and*
rheotropism

chemical composition of water, trout's reactions to,
62, 63

Christian, Herman, 138

chemotropism in trout, 62, 63

chub, 126

closed seasons on fishing, 110

Coffin Fly, 141

color patterns of brown trout,
29–30

colors, distinction of, by trout,
55–56

Compleat Angler, The (Walton),
4 *and n.*

Connett, Eugene V., 124

contact, direct bodily, avoid-
ance of, by trout, 61–62

Cooper, George, 140

Cornell Fish Hatchery Laboratory, 120

Coste, Professor M., 82

Cotton, Charles, 4, 130

Cramp, G. C., 13

Cross, Reuben, 138, 140

Crystal Creek, New York, 66
currents in trout streams, 148–50; *diagram of*, 149
currents, trout's reaction to, 60–61, 63; *diagram of*, 60

dace, black-nosed, 124, 126
Darbee, Elsie, 97, 139
Darbee, Harry, 139, 142, 153
Day, Francis, 33
"deceivers" (dry flies), 140
Deer Creek, Maryland, 113
Delamere, Lord, 13
Delaware River, New York, 95, 122, 128
Dennys, John, 3–4
deterioration and restoration of trout streams, 106–9, 118–19, 125; *diagram of improvements*, 108
Dette, Walt, 138, 138–39, 141
Dette, Winne, 138–39
Deutscher Fischerei Verein, 18
diet of trout, 30, 92–100; in hatcheries, 87–88; other fish in, 124; *chart showing*, 99
digestive system of trout, 40–42; *diagram of*, 41
diseases of trout, 88–91; *chart explaining*, 89
distribution of brown trout, 3, 5, 7–23; *world distribution map*, 10–11
drag in casting, 147, 148, 153
dry flies, 3, 4, 14, 55–56; variety of, 137–43; *diagram of styles*, 137
Dry Fly and Fast Water, The (La Branche), 5
dry-fly fishing, 3, 4, 5, 14, 84, 94–95, 97, 99–100, 113, 114, 128–29 *ff.*

"edge cast," 154
Edwards, Billy, 129
egg predation, 126
eggs, handling, in hatcheries, 84–87; tools for *(diagram)*, 85
eggs, hatching, 85–86; *diagram of*, 86
Ehlinger, Neil F., 27, 38, 39
Elk River (Back Fork), West Virginia, 113, 115
Embody, Dr. George C., 25, 28, 58, 68, 90, 120
Escoffier, Auguste, 2
Esopus River, New York, 95, 122, 128, 130, 140, 141, 153
Europe, distribution of brown trout in, 8
"evening rise," 59, 67, 134
external parasites of trout, 89
eyes of trout, *see* sight, sense of

Fairchild, Julia, 132
fallfish (chub or chavender), 126
Fanwing Royal Coachman, 140–41
fin-clipping as marking device, 27, 156
fingerling stage, 74–75; *diagram of*, 73
fingerlings, diet of, 99
fin rot, 89
fins of brown trout, functions of, 26–28; connection of, to skeleton, 37, *diagram of*, 36
Firehole River, Wyoming, 5
fish hogs, 112–13
fisherman management, 112–13
"fishing-for-fun," 113, 114
Fletcher, Colin, 13, 14, 126

Flick, Arthur A., 98, 125, 138, 140, 142, 148
flies, *see* dry flies *and* dry-fly fishing
flukes (trematodes), 89
Fordridge trout, 30
Francis, Francis, 12
Frost, Dr. W. E., 68
fungus, 25, 84
furunculosis, 89

Game Fish Protection Society, St. Johns, Newfoundland, 21
Garlick, Dr. Theodatus, 82
gas bubble disease, 89
Gehin, Antoine, 82
gillaroo, 30–31, 32
gill disease, 89
gills, structure and function of, 40; *diagram of,* 40
goiter, 89
Gordon, Theodore, 5, 56, 130, 138, 139, 140, 147, 162
Greeley, Dr. John R., 67, 73, 126
Green, Seth, 82–83, 103, 116
Grogan, Major Ewart, 14
Grove, Dr. Alvin R., Jr., 129
growth rates in brown trout, 74–75; differences in, in different waters, 111; *chart showing,* 77
Günther, Dr. A. C. L. C., 31–32
gyrodactylus, 89

Haig-Brown, Roderick L., 138
Halford, Frederic M., 4, 5, 100, 138
handlining, 134
hatcheries, trout in, 12, 13, 18, 21, 59, 68, 79–80, 82, 84–85, 102–3

Jacobi, Stephen Ludwig, 81–82

James, Emerson, 107

Japan, brown trout in, 15

Jennings, Preston J., 98

Jennings, Percy, 142

Johnny darter, 124

Jordan, Wes, 132

Kashmir, introduction of brown trout in, 15

Kennebago River, Maine, 114

Kenya, success of brown trout introduction in, 13–14

La Branche, George M. L., 5, 55, 132, 156

Lac Brule, Quebec, 21

lateral line, 25; as hearing device, 45–46; *diagram of,* 47

Law, Dr. Frank W., 55

Lawson, William, 3

Ledge Pool Brown, 157–60

Leonard, Hiram, 129, 140

life expectancy of trout, 75–76

light, trout's reaction to, 58–60, 156

Light Cahill, 140

lines, 3, 135

Linnaeus, Carl, *Systema Naturae,* 31

live bait, restrictions on, 113

Loch Awe, Scotland, 13

Loch Leven brown trout, 14, 15, 18–19, 21, 31

Loch Lomond, New Brunswick, 21

locomotive mechanism of brown trout, 27–28

Lost Cove Creek, North Carolina, 115

Madagascar, introduction of brown trout in, 15

Madison River, Montana, 5

Manistee River, Michigan, 67

man's aid in spread of brown trout, 8–23, *and see map,* 10–11

Markham, Gervase, 3

marking fish, 27, 156

Mascall, Leonard, 3

Mather, Fred, 15–18, 20, 103, 162

Maturi River, South Island, New Zealand, 13

mayflies, 92, 94, 95–98, 100, 120; dry flies made to emulate, 138, 139–40

migration for spawning, 8, 27, 70, 78

minnow family, 124

Mills, Arthur, 141

Mills, Chester, 140

Mills, Stephen, 141

Mills, Thomas, 140–41

Mohawk River, New York, 79

Montgaudy, Marquis de, 81

Mooi River, Natal, 13

Moore, Dr. Emmeline, 104

Moore, John Trotwood, 60

muscles of trout, 37, 38; eye, 52

mucus, importance of, 25–26

muddler, 61, 124, 126

Nantahala River, North Carolina, 115

Needham, Dr. Paul, 98, 100, 118

negative reactions of fishermen to newly introduced brown trout, 20–21

nesting practices of trout, 70–71, 72

Newman, Ellis, 134, 138, 145, 151

Neversink River, New York, 5, 24, 95, 122, 162

New York State Biological Survey, 104–6

New York State Conservation Department, 83

New York State Fish Commission, 83

New York State Fish Pathology Laboratory, 27, 38

New Zealand, brown trout in, 12, 13

Norfolk, S.S., 12

Notopenis notopenis, 9

nuclear fallout, effect of, in trout streams, 123

nutrition for trout, 103

Otis, Maurice B., 107

oxygen, mechanism of trout's use of, 39–40

Paloot, Terry, 137, 153

parasitic infections, 90; *diagram of*, 89

parr marks, 28–29; *diagram showing*, 73

Payne, Ed, 129–30

Payne, Jim, 130

Pere Marquette River, Michigan, 18, 67

pesticides in trout streams, dangers of, 123

pH readings in trout streams, 121–22

Phillipe, Samuel, 129

phototropism in trout, 58–60, 156

Pinchon, Dom, 81, 103

Plenty River, Tasmania, 12

popeye disease, 64

prehistory of brown trout, 8, 25

Puerto Rico, introduction of brown trout in, 17

Pulman, George P. R., 4

"quality fishing," 102–3, 109–10, 112, 114–15

Quill Gordon, 139

rainbow trout, 30, 120

Rangely River, Maine, 114

Rat Faced McDougall, 142

rattailed maggot, 120–21

redd, *see* nesting practices

reels, 3, 133–34

regulations governing public fishing, 110–13, 115, 125

Remy, Joseph, 82

reproduction in brown trout, 67–73

retractor lentis muscle, 52

rheotropism, 60–61, 63; *diagram of*, 60

"ringers," 84

rising trout, indications of, to fisherman, 145–46

Ritz, Charles, 132

rods for trout fishing, development of modern, 3, 4, 129–33

Roeliff Jansen Kill, New York, 150

Ronalds, Alfred, 98

Rondout Creek, New York, 5, 95, 119, 122, 128, 133, 155, 162

Roosevelt, Theodore, 83–84

roundworms (nematodes), 89

salmon, 20, 30

salmon eggs, transplanting of, 9–12

salmon-trout, 30

San Juan River, New Mexico, 115

Savage River, Maryland, 113, 115

scales, development of, 25, 75; *diagram showing,* 76

Schmidt, J., 37

Schoharie Creek, New York, 95, 125

Schubert, Franz, 2

sculpin (muddler), 61, 124, 126

sea trout, 8, 22, 26, 30, 33, 43, 49

sexual development in trout, 68–69, 76–78

sexual intercourse in trout, 72

sexual maturity, 111

Shavers Fork, West Virginia, 113, 115

sight, sense of, in trout, 44, 40–56; *diagrams explaining,* 51, 53, 54

siltation, destructive effects of, 106, 107, 109

size limits, validity of, 110–12, 115

skeletal structure of brown trout, 35–37; *diagram of,* 36

skin covering the scales, 25

smell, sense of, in trout, 44, 48–50; *diagram of nostrils,* 49

Smith, Ray, 138, 148, 152, 153, 154

Société Zoologique d'acclimation de Paris, 81

South Africa, establishment of brown trout in, 13

South America, brown trout in, 22

South Mills River, North Carolina, 115

spawning, 67 *ff.*

Spring Creek, Pennsylvania, 113

Steenrod, Roy, 130, 138, 139, 140

Stevenson, George, 130

stiff hackle on dry flies, 153

stocking of streams, failures in, 103–4, 105

stripping trout of spawn, 80–81

sucker, 126

Tåning, A. V., 37

tapered fly lines, 134–35

tapeworms (cestodes), 89

Tasmania, brown trout established in, 12, 13

Tarzwell, Dr. Clarence M., 107

teeth, vomerine, 30, 32

temperature of water, effect of, on trout body structure, 37; on heartbeat, 38–39; *diagram of,* 39

Tenmile River, New York, 93

Test River, England, 9

thermal shock, 63

thermotropism in trout, 62–64

thigotropism in trout, 61–62

Thomas, Fred, 129

Thomas, Captain Terry B., 135

touch, sense of, in trout, 46–48

Townsend, Ted, 141

Treatyse of Fysshynge with an Angle (Berners), 3

Trewavas, Dr., 33

trichodina, 89

Trimm, Wayne, 2

trimming flies, 152

trophy trout waters, 115–16

trout eggs, transplanting of, 12 *ff.*

"trout stamp," 113–14

"trout's window," 54–55, 155
"tummy tickling," 48

ulcers, 89
Umgeni River, Natal, 13
United States Fish Commission, 16, 18

Van Dyke, Henry, 133
varieties of brown trout, 14, 15, 18, 30–33
vertebrae, variable number of, in trout skeleton, 36–37
von Behr, Baron Lucius, 18
von Behr trout, 31

Walton, Izaak, 4 *and n.*, 8, 29, 30, 61, 98, 117, 126, 132

water quality necessary for trout streams, 119, 120–22
Waters Creek, Georgia, 115
Westman, Dr. James R., 23
Wetzel, Charles, M., 98
Willowemoc River, New York, 95, 112, 113, 128
Wilson Creek, North Carolina, 115
"winter band" on scales, 75
"winter kill," 123
Wolf, Dr. Louis, 38, 90
Wolf River, Wisconsin, 5
Woman Flyfisher's Club, 132

Yellow Breeches Creek, Pennsylvania, 115

The Compleat Brown Trout